WISDOM
IN THE
WOUND

WISDOM
IN THE
WOUND

How God Uses Your Past
to Shape Who You're Becoming

TONY MILTENBERGER

invite
PRESS
Plano, Texas

WISDOM IN THE WOUND
How God Uses Your Past to Shape Who You're Becoming

Copyright ©2025 by Tony Miltenberger

This book is printed on acid-free, elemental chlorine-free paper.

ISBN Paperback: 9781963265606; eBook: 9781963265613

All Scripture quotations unless noted otherwise are taken from taken from THE HOLY BIBLE, NEW INTERNATIONAL VERSION®, NIV® Copyright © 1973, 1978, 1984, 2011 by Biblica, Inc.™ Used by permission of Zondervan. All rights reserved worldwide.

Scripture quotations marked (NLT) are taken from the Holy Bible, New Living Translation, copyright ©1996, 2004, 2015 by Tyndale House Foundation. Used by permission of Tyndale House Publishers, Carol Stream, Illinois 60188. All rights reserved.

25 26 27 28 29 30 31 32 33 34—10 9 8 7 6 5 4 3 2 1

MANUFACTURED in the UNITED STATES of AMERICA

To my incredible parents — thank you for the foundation of love, faith, and strength you gave me. Your consistent presence, wise guidance, and willingness to surround me with mentors shaped who I am. Your love has always been both a safety net and a launching pad.

To Connor, Caleb, and Shiloh — thank you for the gift of your stories and the courage to let me share even the hard parts. Being your dad is one of the greatest honors of my life. Walking alongside you is one of my deepest joys.

To my amazing wife, Karen — thank you for growing up with me. Sharing life with my best friend has made every challenge worth facing and every milestone even sweeter.

"Now to him who is able to do immeasurably more than all we ask or imagine, according to his power that is at work within us."
— Ephesians 3:20

This book is a reminder that pain doesn't get the last word. Tony shows us that our wounds aren't meant to be hidden or ignored; they are an invitation to get to work. If you have been wondering whether your story still matters, this book will be a reminder that it does.

—**Bob Goff**, New York Times bestselling author of
Love Does and *Undistracted*

Contents

Foreword

When someone sees you, not just your work, or your accomplishments, or the ideas you bring to the table, but *you*, it feels holy. There's a sort of undefinable sacred connection that happens when someone is curious about who you are and what makes you tick. That's what it feels like to have a conversation with Tony.

He doesn't just ask questions. He listens with the kind of attunement that makes you feel safe enough to tell the truth. About your faith. About your doubts. About your wounds. He's one of the few people I know who can hold space for both the mess and the miracle without rushing you to resolve either. He's spent years helping others name what aches in them, and now, in this book, he offers that same presence, that same gentleness, to readers.

Wisdome in the Wound is not just a book about wounds—it's a book about the wisdom we gain from tending them. It's about the gifts that live on the other side of the pain we've spent years trying to ignore, minimize, or outrun. Tony writes with vulnerability, insight, and an unwavering pastoral heart to help walk us through how our earliest experiences of hurt become the filter through which we interpret the world. And how, by bringing those wounds into the light, we can find healing, not only for ourselves but for the people we love and lead.

This book doesn't demand that you be unbreakable. In fact, it's a pretty compelling argument for why you *shouldn't* be. Instead, Tony gives us language for our humanity, permission for our grief, and a gentle push toward healing, not perfection. And maybe most importantly, he reminds us that courage isn't the absence of pain. Courage is what happens when we choose to face our pain with compassion, curiosity, and hope.

If you've ever felt stuck in the story of your own brokenness, if you've wondered whether your wound disqualifies you from being a good parent, leader, friend, or follower of Jesus, this book is for you. And Tony is the perfect guide for the journey.

You'll feel seen and safe as you read, and if you're willing, you just might come away believing that the wound you carry doesn't have the final word.

Kristen LaValley, author of *Even if He Doesn't: What We Believe About God When Life Doesn't Make Sense*

Introduction

It was about fifteen minutes into our second walk of the day when I had an intense feeling of déjà vu—not in the physical sense but in the emotional. I had been in this same emotional position before, and the flood of feelings was all too familiar. I remember the day vividly: a beautiful spring afternoon in Ohio, my family of five walking through the neighborhood, trying to shake off the weight of uncertainty that had become a defining part of our lives. These walks were a necessity. They were our way of escaping the oppressive stillness that had settled over everything. My wife and I walked side by side, talking, while our kids played ahead. Yet, despite the joy of seeing them carefree for a moment, I couldn't escape the lingering heaviness. COVID-19 had gripped our entire country, and it was a difficult season.

This wasn't the first time I'd felt trapped in a feeling of déjà vu that I couldn't seem to break, no matter how hard I tried. The first time came years earlier, during the summer of 2005. I was three months into a twelve-month deployment at Camp Doha, Kuwait. Life there revolved around a monotonous cycle of work, walks outside, and waiting. Waiting for change, waiting for something to break the endless repetition. Deployment life is a strange existence. It's a mix of routine and high-stakes tension, of waiting for the unpredictable while enduring the unchanging.

Each day carried a weight of its own, an unshakable sense of sameness. Yet, in the midst of that monotony, there was also an underlying tension. You knew change could come at any moment, but until then, you were stuck. It felt like being anchored in the middle of a storm, unable to move but bracing for impact. That experience shaped me in ways I couldn't fully appreciate at the time. It taught me how life's rhythms often intertwine routine with upheaval, sometimes so seamlessly that we barely notice the transition until we're already in it.

Walking through my neighborhood years later during the COVID-19 pandemic brought those memories rushing back. In May 2020, the world felt unrecognizable, yet the emotional terrain was all too familiar. The déjà vu was a similar feeling of prolonged stress brought on by a situation that felt outside my control and (at times) overwhelming. The prolonged stress of the pandemic mirrored my deployment in unsettling ways. COVID-19 was the deployment no one asked for, and yet here we all were, grappling with uncertainty, isolation, and an unrelenting sense of waiting. Unlike the military, however, most of us lacked the systems or training to cope with the impact of prolonged stress. We didn't have the tools or support structures to process what was happening, let alone to understand how it was reshaping us.

That's the thing about prolonged stress: It doesn't just weigh on you in the moment; it lingers. Over time, it turns the cracks in our lives into canyons. Cracks are the small, manageable fractures we can ignore or step over. But canyons? They demand our attention. They force us to stop, to look down into their depths, and to reckon with what we see. They reveal parts of ourselves we might prefer to leave hidden. Yet, as inconvenient as these canyons may be, they offer us a gift—the opportunity to understand ourselves more deeply and to grow.

As I reflect on these canyons—those deep emotional spaces shaped by prolonged stress and wounds—I am reminded that my faith journey didn't begin in adulthood. It started in the tumultuous years of my adolescence. When I was 16, anger seemed to define me. I struggled to control it, lashing out at the world around me, even those who cared for me the most. It felt like I was trapped in an emotional storm with no way out, like I was constantly teetering on the edge of a canyon I couldn't see the bottom of.

Looking back, I know that I wouldn't have survived that season without faith—and without the people God placed in my life to guide me. My parents, my youth pastor, my local parish priest, and others from my church saw something in me that I couldn't yet see in myself. They didn't just give me advice; they walked with me through the mess. They showed me patience when I didn't deserve it, grace when I lashed out, and love when I felt unlovable.

It wasn't an instant transformation. Faith doesn't work like a light switch, flipping everything from dark to light in a single moment. But it was faith—both my fledgling faith in Jesus and the steadfast faith others had in me—that began to soften the hard edges of my anger. It taught me to trust that there was a purpose even in my pain. Through that trust, I began to see that I wasn't defined by my failures or my struggles.

That experience taught me an important truth: Healing doesn't happen in isolation. God often works through the people around us, through community, to bring about the transformation we so desperately need. Faith was the bridge that helped me cross the canyon of my own anger. It gave me the courage to face the emotions I had buried deep within and to believe that I could be more than the sum of my mistakes. That bridge of faith was shown to me by God, but stewarded by having people in my life who could help me see a different version of myself and help guide me across that bridge of faith. Walking with God is a walk that we were never meant to take on our own; it was always meant to be done in community. We serve a God who cares deeply about us and gives us the Body of Christ (the people) to live out our faith together.

As I've grown older, I've carried that lesson with me, though I didn't always recognize it at the time. Faith isn't just the solution to one particular struggle; it's the foundation that steadies us when life shakes us to our core. When I walked through the neighborhood during those long days of the pandemic, feeling the weight of stress and uncertainty pressing down on me, I realized that same faith—the one that carried me through my anger at 16—was still carrying me. And just as God had placed people in my life to guide me then, He was still doing the same, using the community around me to remind me that I wasn't alone

Looking back, I realize that the feelings I experienced both during those neighborhood walks in 2020 and in my adolescent anger were a confrontation with the canyons in my own life, the wounds that had been opened by prolonged stress and left to linger. Those wounds, shaped by both the extraordinary and the mundane, had become part of who I was. They influenced how I led, how I loved, and how I lived.

If you're holding this book, it's likely because you too have experienced these canyons. Maybe you've noticed the cracks in your life deepening under the weight of stress, or perhaps you've felt the pull to explore the depths of your own experiences. Either way, my prayer is that this book will serve as a guide for your journey. Together, we'll explore wounds that shape us, prolonged stress that transforms us, and ways we can emerge stronger on the other side.

Let me be clear: I have never met a person who hasn't been impacted by wounds. Some are easy to identify, like the scars left by significant trauma or loss. Others are more subtle, borne from the quiet accumulation of life's stresses and disappointments. These wounds often feel like invisible weights, burdens we carry without fully understanding their origins. For many, it's as if a giant wound lives on their chest, always present, sometimes flaring up in the most unexpected ways.

Acknowledging these wounds can be overwhelming, even frightening. But it's also the first step toward healing. As you read through these pages, I want to encourage you: If what you uncover feels too heavy to carry alone, do not hesitate to seek help. Whether it's a pastor, a trusted friend, or a mental health professional, having someone to walk alongside you can make all the difference. Since 2012, I've routinely seen a counselor, and it's a practice I wouldn't trade for anything. There's immense value in having a safe space to process the complexities of life and leadership. Even now as an executive coach, pastor, and leader, having someone to talk to in my own life is incredibly important as I process this thing we call life.

This type of work—the work of facing our wounds and stepping into healing—is profoundly meaningful, yet it's unlike almost any other endeavor we undertake. It's not about measurable achievements or visible milestones; it's about developing the soft skills that shape the very core of who we are. The ability to sit with discomfort, to name our pain, to seek forgiveness, or to extend grace—all of these require courage and a willingness to step into vulnerability. These aren't the kind of skills you list on a résumé, yet they are foundational to living a life of depth, connection, and purpose. Unlike a project with a clear start and finish, this work is ongoing and deeply personal. It requires patience, self-compassion, and a commitment to growth, even when the results aren't immediately apparent. But make no mistake: The transformation it brings is invaluable, impacting not only how we lead and live but also how we love and serve those around us.

At the core of this book is my belief in the transformative power of faith. My relationship with Jesus has been the foundation of every good thing in my life; as the psalmist declares, *"Unless the LORD builds the house, the builders labor in vain"* (Psalm 127:1). Following Him has revealed the depth of my wounds while also offering the hope of redemption, a truth echoed in 2 Corinthians 12:9: *"My grace is sufficient for you, for my power is made perfect in weakness."* If faith in Jesus isn't a part of your life right now, that's okay. The truths about wounds, healing, and growth are universal. My hope is that this book will still serve you well, providing tools and perspectives to navigate your own journey toward healing and wholeness.

One of the most profound truths I've learned is this: On the other side of our wounds lies our greatest gift. It's a paradox that often feels counterintuitive. How can something born out of pain become something beautiful? Yet, time and again, I've seen this truth play out—in my own life and in the lives of others. The very wounds that threaten to define us can become the source of our greatest strength, compassion, and purpose. This is the redemptive power of God at work, turning what was meant for harm into something good.

Prolonged stress, wounds, and canyons—these are realities we all face. But they are not the end of the story. They are the beginning of a deeper understanding of who we are and who we are called to be. My prayer is that this book will serve as a companion on your journey, offering insights, encouragement, and perhaps a new perspective on the art of living and leading with grace.

This book was written with leaders in mind, but I believe leadership happens on many levels. One of my core beliefs is that leadership is about influence, and because we all have a community, that means every single one of us is a leader in some capacity. We don't all lead in the same way, and you don't have to identify as a traditional leader to recognize the impact you have. Leadership isn't reserved for CEOs, pastors, or managers; it's woven into our everyday interactions. If you have family, friends, or a job, you are already shaping the world around you. Some lead by example, others lead through encouragement, and still others lead by offering wisdom or support. Whether you are guiding a family, supporting friends, or making decisions in the workplace, your presence and actions influence those around you. So, the question isn't whether or not you are a leader; the question is how you are leading. My hope is that this book will help you become more aware of the ways your personal journey—your wounds, your growth, and your healing—can positively impact those who look to you, whether you realize it or not.

I want to leave you with a promise and a challenge. The promise is this: You are not alone. Your wounds, no matter how deep, do not have the final word. There is hope, there is healing, and there is a gift waiting on the other side. The challenge is to approach this journey with courage and openness. Allow yourself to feel, to question, and to grow. Be willing to sit with the discomfort and to confront the parts of yourself that you've avoided. Growth is rarely easy, but it is always worth it.

So, let's begin. Together, let's explore the depths of our canyons and discover the gifts waiting on the other side. Let's confront our wounds, not with fear but with faith and courage. And let's remember that even in our brokenness, there is beauty, and even in our pain, there is purpose. May this journey bring you closer to the truth of who you are and the God who loves you more than you can imagine. Be courageous; your greatest gift is waiting.

Chapter 1

Your Wound

Now the serpent was more crafty than any of the wild animals the LORD God had made. He said to the woman, "Did God really say, 'You must not eat from any tree in the garden'?"

– Genesis 3:1

"The epistemic consequence of sin." When Dr. David Watson first used this phrase in my life, I had to do a double take. I remember sitting in his class while attending United Theological Seminary and as I wrote it down, I immediately felt in over my head. Such a big term, and not a term I had ever used before. I did what every good student does in preparation for a term he/she doesn't understand—I Googled it.

The Google search wasn't extremely helpful, and amid my own discovery (and through conversation with Dr. Watson), I came up with my working definition—the epistemic consequence of sin is the sin that exists in the world because of the very nature of brokenness in the world. It's the brokenness of humanity. And as long as you are a resident of the world, you experience the consequences of that brokenness. It might also be helpful to define what "sin" is, as we all come from different backgrounds. *Sin* is anything that separates us from God. Some of that separation is because of my choices, some of that separation is generational choices, and the sin I am specifically referencing here is a direct result of the brokenness in the world. When Adam and Eve ate the fruit, they were kicked out of the Garden, and that is when the epistemic consequence of sin began. Not attempting to reduce the consequences of sin, but in the effort of making it palatable, it works the same way it worked when I was a kid. As a kid, if I made a choice that hurt my brothers or sisters, there were always consequences, and oftentimes that consequence might be sitting on the steps or writing an apology note.

While it is easy to think of the epistemic consequence of sin as a theological construct, it is far more relational than that. Whether in your family, your workplace, or your friend group, when we separate ourselves from God, there is a consequence, and it is impossible to avoid. Since the beginning of time, people have been hurting others and recovering from the consequences of that action. Even if you don't believe in God, think of the relational context that sin represents separation—we separate ourselves from other people and even our own values. Sin equals separation.

Super uplifting way to start a book, right? Well, this is important when it comes to your wounding. The wound is part of that sin-consequence. In psychological terms, it is often referred to as "little t" trauma. This concept has its roots in trauma research, particularly the work of clinicians like Bessel van der Kolk (*The Body Keeps the Score*) and Peter Levine (*Waking the Tiger*), who emphasize the cumulative impact of smaller, non-life-threatening events on emotional well-being. Little "t" trauma is part of what it means to be human, and I have yet to find a human who doesn't have it.

Essentially, a wound becomes the filter through which you experience life. It colors your thoughts, emotions, and actions in ways that are often subtle but deeply impactful. Whether you acknowledge it or not, it's always there, shaping how you interact with the world and with others. It influences your decisions, how you respond to challenges, and even how you interpret moments of joy or conflict. The reality is, no matter how much we might try to compartmentalize or push it aside, the wound is woven into the fabric of our lives, affecting every relationship we're in and every endeavor we pursue. It's as if it's part of our very being.

Most of the people I work with (in all walks of life, from being a stay at home parent to a leader in the most traditional sense) carry wounds that trace back to their formative years, typically between the ages of 4 and 12. These are the years when our understanding of the world begins to take shape, and we start to make sense of our relationships, our surroundings, and, most importantly, our sense of self. During this critical developmental window, we are highly impressionable. We absorb not only what is said but also what is left unsaid. Actions, inactions, tone, and even silence become the building blocks of our perception of love, safety, and belonging.

It is in these moments, often without anyone intending harm, that small "t" trauma takes root. Small "t" trauma doesn't arise from dramatic, life-altering events (although it can certainly be influenced by those events); rather, it comes from the ordinary, everyday experiences that leave an unintended mark. Maybe a parent's busy schedule made you feel unseen, a teacher's critical comment made you question your abilities, or a friend's rejection caused you to doubt your worth. These moments, though seemingly minor at the time, begin to accumulate. They shape the stories we tell ourselves about who we are and how much we matter.

The heartbreaking reality is that in small "t" trauma, there is no villain. No one sets out with the intention of wounding. Parents, teachers, and caregivers are often doing the best they can with the resources they have. Yet, despite their best efforts, children can interpret the actions of trusted adults in their lives or lack of actions—in ways that feel hurtful. A scolding meant to teach a lesson can be received as rejection. A missed event due to work commitments can be seen as abandonment. A well-meaning attempt to "toughen up" a child can feel like a lack of love.

These experiences leave invisible imprints on our hearts, shaping how we see ourselves and how we relate to others. The child who feels unseen may grow into an adult who craves constant affirmation. The child who felt rejected may become an adult who avoids vulnerability at all costs. These wounds, formed unintentionally in childhood, carry forward into adulthood, influencing relationships, careers, and even faith.

Acknowledging the existence of these wounds is the first step toward healing. It allows us to move past blame and toward understanding—understanding that the pain is real but so is the opportunity for growth. It's an invitation to rewrite the narratives we've carried for years and to replace them with truths rooted in love, grace, and hope.

For me, this wound takes the form of an amoeba-like shape that lives on my chest. In my mind's eye, it has rough, uneven edges and a muted, almost dull appearance—not particularly attractive yet unmistakably present. It's not something I chose, but over time, I've come to see it as a kind of badge of honor. It represents the battles I've fought, the struggles I've endured, and the resilience I've gained along the way. It's a reminder that I've survived, even when the odds felt insurmountable. With time and courage, the wound you are carrying will stop being scary and start being a part of who you are with grace. Grace is best described as "unmerited favor." As we think about our wounds, how amazing would it be to think that even in something that was once painful can now be seen as a pretty incredible part of how God uses your story—His unmerited favor.

This wound doesn't just exist passively—it rolls with us through life, shifting and changing with our circumstances. Certain situations, interactions, or even seemingly random triggers can make it throb with fresh pain. A difficult conversation with a coworker, a moment of vulnerability with a spouse, or even a fleeting memory can awaken it, reminding you of the depth of its presence. Yet, while it can be painful, it also serves as a source of perspective. It reminds me that healing is not a straight line but a journey, and the wound, though ever-present, doesn't define my story. Instead, it invites me to acknowledge its presence, tend to its edges, and live with intentionality in the tension between pain and growth.

Let me be clear about something: I've done hundreds of counseling sessions with people of all ages, races, and walks of life, and I have never found anyone who doesn't have a wound. Sure, you may not be able to identify it (yet), you may not know its edges, you may not even be able to look at it but let me assure you—you've been wounded. The sooner you come to that conclusion the sooner you can begin to become self-aware and grow in wisdom. Coming to that conclusion is an opportunity to put words and handles around something that may have previously felt unmanageable. Coming to grips with the wound would be akin to holding water in your hands cupped together—it's not perfect, but it is a great way to get the drink you desperately crave. For many of us, our wound is a stumbling block until we know it well enough that it doesn't cause us to stumble. Intimacy with our wound leads to the gift of wisdom and growth.

Your wound is how you feel through the world. It becomes a lens of sorts but an emotional lens. As you interact with people, as you lead people, as you parent little people—all of it is impacted by your wound. I think it's part of the reason why the most intimate relationships hurt the most because they have access to the wound in a way others don't. No one can cause me to lose my cool like my kids... one eye roll, one sarcastic remark, one of anything, and suddenly my emotional intensity spikes to an unhealthy place. It happens to all of us, and yet, for most of us, we never spend time exploring what that means. We never spend time getting to know the edges of our wound. Because of that willful ignorance, we don't know when we are making decisions from a place of woundedness, and we certainly don't know when someone/something is bumping up against it. The best comparison I can make is the image of walking through your bedroom in the middle of the night in complete darkness, knowing that 535 Legos are lying on the floor. As you make the trek to the bathroom, you know they are out there; you just don't know when (or if) you'll step on one. Most of us go through life like the image of the Lego blocks... they are out there; we just don't know when we'll step on one. And very few things in life hurt as much as stepping on a Lego in a pitch-black room during the middle of the night.

Where does the wound come from? Well, remember, it is the epistemic consequence of sin—it's the brokenness of the world.

The wound that comes from the epistemic consequence of sin is not big "T" trauma; instead, it is little "t" trauma or an accumulation of pain that you experienced growing up. And, for the sake of clarity, a lot of humans must wrestle with both wounding and big "T" trauma, and if that's you—I'm sorry. It's incredibly hard. Big "T" trauma is usually a defining moment in your life, and it is always an excruciating event (that's what makes it traumatic). Big "T" trauma is something like sexual assault, watching your parents get divorced, addiction, and countless other events that happen to people every single day. Big "T" trauma requires real help, and if you've experienced any of that in your life, let me encourage you to get some help. Find someone in your world who can walk with you through that pain. Little "t" trauma is a little different.

This is what I refer to as your wound. Your wound is harder to identify; it's harder to get your hands/mind around. It is more a result of an upbringing or a slant on the way your parents raised you in the world. It is little things played out over time, accumulating pain and influencing how you give and receive love.

Let me give you an example: When I moved to Centerville, Ohio, I did so as the lead pastor of a local church. I was so excited when my wife agreed to the move; this was going to be a big career move for me. It was a church that was older and open to the revitalization work that I loved to be a part of. I was so excited—I knew God was going to move mountains! My oldest son (Connor) was eight and he was such a joy to have around. He was a part of my ministry, and the entire church loved having him around. It had been so long since they had a pastor with kids that every time I brought him to something, I got kudos or additional support. Connor was such an important part of the success I witnessed in the church. Young(ish) pastor with young kids, doing all the things in the church and in the community. Can you imagine being a church kid? Well, one of the things that happens to church kids is that they are told to behave a certain way. And to be clear, my son is great (he has since graduated high school)—he has always made responsible choices and isn't the cliche of a pastor's kid. Yet, in those formative years, I had an expectation of him; I need you here, I need you to act a certain way, I need you to stand by my side or else we may not be successful. Also, we lived in the church parsonage (think house for the pastor), so in some sense, my entire family felt like if I got fired, we may not have a place to live. All of that impacted my son, and my son's wound is that he feels pressured to perform to receive my love. Now, did I do this on purpose? NO! Do I want this for his life? Absolutely not. Is there anything I can do to fix it? Nope! Having the opportunity to discuss this reality with him has helped me understand him as a man, and while I hate it for him, the truth is—it just comes with being human. I was doing the best I could with what I had, and so was he.

Most wounds come from an interpretation of a situation that was unintended and is just a result of brokenness. There was never a day where I woke up and said, "Today is the day I want to wound my son" (or anyone else for that matter). As a parent, my intentions were always grounded in love and care—I wanted the best for my children. Yet, intentions don't always protect against impact. While it is not my fault (meaning it's not a direct causation) that he is wounded, it doesn't make it hurt any less. The hurt is real, and that's part of the brokenness of the world. It's a strange tension to sit in, knowing you've done your best, yet realizing your best wasn't enough to prevent pain. I own the unintended consequences of my actions and owning it might be as simple as acknowledging there is pain. I don't have to fix it in order to acknowledge it.

The brokenness of the world has a way of creating cracks even in the most loving relationships. Sometimes, those cracks form because of miscommunication or unmet expectations—small, seemingly insignificant moments that lodge themselves deep in the heart. Other times, it's the absence of something, like a hug that wasn't given, a word of encouragement that wasn't said, or a moment that slipped away unnoticed. These moments are not deliberate acts of harm; they were often byproducts of fatigue, distraction, or simply not knowing what was needed in the moment. No one's fault, no malice intended, just a consequence of the world's brokenness.

And yet, despite the lack of intent, the pain is real. It lingers in the heart of the one who experienced it, shaping how they view themselves and the world. This is how wounds work. As I mentioned earlier, they usually form somewhere between the ages of 4 and 12, during the formative years when we're interpreting everything around us through the limited lens of childhood. Cracks are the spaces that eventually lead to the pain points that penetrate the heart. It is important to remember this because when you start thinking about your own wound, this is the timeframe in your life you'll want to zero in on. Those interpretations you had as a child become truths that we carry, often without realizing it. These wounds then stick with us as a lens through which we feel and experience the world for the rest of our lives. Think about the lens as a kaleidoscope. Every crack, every relationship, and every experience turns together in a way that impacts how we see the world. They color our relationships, our reactions, and even our sense of self-worth, leaving us to navigate life with the challenge of carrying a pain that was never intended but is nonetheless deeply felt.

For the record, wounds don't go away, but we do learn to live with them (more about this later), and we learn that on the other side of our wounds is almost always our greatest gift. Most people I talk to about the concept of wounds struggle with this because a lot of us wrestle with the uncomfortable truth that there is hurting in the world, and we can't do anything to stop it. Even more unsettling is the realization that our kids, our spouses, and those closest to us might be hurting because of something we did or didn't do. That reality is hard to sit with, and it can leave us feeling powerless, guilty, or overwhelmed. The only way I've learned to deal with this reality is to surrender those feelings and situations to the Lord. My faith has been a huge gift to me in this process. I know that I inadvertently hurt people and that those actions have led to wounding—yet, I take comfort in my faith which says that there is grace. Grace for me and grace for the person who is hurt. Knowing that it is impossible to live in this broken world and not be hurt has helped me be okay with just being me to the best of my ability.

Relationships, especially intimate ones like marriage or parenting, are never void of hurt. The closer you get to someone (spouse, kids, friends) the more access that person (spouse, kids, friends) has to your wounds and the more likely you are to hurt those close people in your life unintentionally. It's not a question of if but when. This isn't a failure; it's simply part of being human. Loving deeply means opening yourself to both the joy and the pain of connection. You are going to hurt the people you love, not because you want to but because you're imperfect. This truth doesn't mean we stop trying to do better; rather, it invites us to extend grace—to others and to ourselves—when the inevitable happens.

Scripture consistently reflects this reality of human imperfection and the need for grace. In Romans 3:23, Paul reminds us, "For all have sinned and fall short of the glory of God." This is a universal truth: No one is without fault, and our imperfection impacts those around us. Yet, the same chapter gives us hope as Paul continues in Romans 3:24, "and all are justified freely by his grace through the redemption that came by Christ Jesus." Grace is the bridge that covers the gap between our imperfections and God's standard of love.

This is the reality of this side of heaven, and until Jesus comes back, nothing is going to stop that pattern. What we can do, however, is learn from the hurt, grow through the hurt, and allow God to redeem it. In Ephesians 4:32, we are called to, *"Be kind and compassionate to one another, forgiving each other, just as in Christ God forgave you."* This verse underscores the importance of extending forgiveness, not only to others but also to ourselves as an act of grace that mirrors God's own forgiveness.

Jesus is the perfect example of truth and grace. In being like Jesus, I know I do the most good I can while hurting the least amount of people. His example shows us what it means to lead and love. Even though we will never be perfect, we can reflect His love and strive to repair the wounds we cause, trusting that His grace is sufficient for the gaps we can't fill (2 Corinthians 12:9).

Let's take another example of how wounds form and how they impact our lives. And for the sake of transparency, I'll use my own life.

When I was four years old, my parents had unplanned twins. I can remember the day mom went into labor; we were at my dad's company picnic. My dad yelled so loud for my sister and me to get in the back of the station wagon that I ran faster than I can ever remember. My younger brother and sister (the twins) are two of the most incredible humans I know. They are caring, loving, and creative. They have beautiful families, and if they weren't in my life, I would be devastated. Also, their arrival into my life had a direct impact on me. When they came home from the hospital, I didn't know my life would change forever. I went from being the youngest to the middle, and it would set me down on a course that would leave me feeling like I wasn't seen. Classic middle child syndrome, I immediately felt like I didn't matter to the important people in my life, and while in hindsight I know that wasn't true, it felt so real to me. Through no one's fault, no one's malice, no one's intended harm—I began to feel like I didn't matter. This became my wound. It was later reinforced when my parents got divorced and again reinforced when both my parents found new spouses. And again—no one did this to me—this is just a result of brokenness in the world. My parents anguished over how to raise four kids; they did the absolute best they could. And I came out wounded. As a young man, I watched my parents do things that were the right decision for them with all the information that was available to them at the time. They made good choices, and the brokenness of the world still happened to me. It has probably happened to you as well. Learning the edges of my wound has given me a deeper and stronger relationship with my parents. Navigating which part of my feelings are just my interpretation of the situation versus the intent of the situation is a life-changing gift. As you begin to feel the edges of your wound, you'll notice a sense of freedom, understanding that no one "did this" to you, but instead, it's just a reality of how you see the world.

If you happen to be a parent and you are reading this, let me assure you of something—you have wounded your kids. You didn't do it on purpose, you didn't do it with malice, and they are most definitely wounded. Wounds are a result of the brokenness of humanity, so as long as you are raising humans, you are faced with the same reality as the rest of us. I have yet to find a parent who hasn't wounded their kids. Chasing after perfection when it comes to raising children can sometimes become an idol in your life. I've met tons of parents who listen to their kids far more than they listen to their spouse or even God. Parenting isn't about perfection; it is about loving our kids the best way we know how and realizing that the relationship can last for their lifetime. Let me also assure you of this: *In the brokenness of the world, we find God's redemption and grace.* The journey of following Jesus is rooted in this redemption. Release the idea that you can be a perfect parent, and instead embrace the idea that your kids already have a Savior… and it's not you.

God's gifts are waiting for us on the other side of our wound. It is there and unfailing. God shows up for every one of us. One of the realities I have learned to face in doing this work is that I cannot be the savior of my kids (or the people I lead). What I can do is give them the tools to root themselves in something that is bigger than they are and bigger than their wounds, showing them that the wound doesn't have the final say. My parents did this for me; they made me get active in a Christian community and surrounded me with people who could help reinforce the direction they wanted for my life. Even amid their own divorce, they would all (my parents and their spouses) meet to discuss the kids (namely me), and in that discussion, they would acknowledge the situation they were in as they made steps to move it towards a desired outcome. They gave me the tools to see myself in something bigger than our house, our situation, or my wound—we are here today because they did that. I can say that the work I get to do is because God has redeemed my wound, and God used my parents in that process as well.

Your wound is a part of your life; it is part of the life of every human you know, and the gift of wisdom is becoming so familiar with the wound that it no longer has the authority to make decisions in your life. The reason we must start the journey off by talking about the hard stuff is that it is the only way to get a clear picture of where you are. More often than not, we have a tendency to over-romanticize the reality of the situation. In other words, when it comes to our own brokenness, we put on rose colored glasses. Over the next couple of chapters, we are going to help you find your wound, we are going to help you touch it, and we are going to go down a path that just maybe makes it seem a little less scary. What you will need is courage: courage to do the deep work, courage to sit in your feelings, and courage to understand this is hard and that's okay. Being courageous is taking the time to hold that wound with love and respect so that you can hold other people the way God intended.

Exercise:

1. **Journaling Prompt:** Reflect on an experience that may have shaped a significant part of your life. What do you feel as you reflect on those experiences? Sometimes emotions can be hard to name; if you are struggling with the types of emotions, take some time to google "feeling word sheet," and you will find a tool to help you call out the feelings around those past experiences.

2. **Emotional Awareness:** Thinking about the kaleidoscope lens of your life, where has it caused you to see the world differently? For example, what relationships have been impacted by those wounds?

3. **Challenge:** Talk to your parents or a sibling about what it was like growing up and what you think your wound might be. Be open and ask good questions. Take the opportunity to learn that maybe your way of seeing things isn't the only way to see things.

Chapter 2

How Do You Know What Your Wound Is?

"Who told you that you were naked?" the LORD God asked.
— Genesis 3:11a (NLT)

The term "self-aware" has never sat well with me. The truth is, I never felt unaware, I never felt like I wasn't in touch with myself, and I never thought I didn't know what was happening to me emotionally. Dr. John Van Epp wrote a book called *How to Avoid Marrying a Jerk*. He would define the term "jerk" by saying that a jerk is someone who doesn't know that they have a problem. I have been a jerk many times in my life. Like many things, we don't know what we don't know. I wish there was a simpler way to say it or a better understanding of how it all worked, but until you go searching for something, it's challenging to find anything. For many of us, the journey to deeper self-understanding didn't start till we were forced to look for it. The same is true with our wound. Until you make the conscious choice to go down the road, you won't find out what your wound is or how it works in your life.

The problem with searching for the wound is that you'll often bump up against a lot of things that aren't the wound but still feel painful. In some ways, it's like trying to find the light switch in a pitch-black space (remember the 535 Legos on the floor?!). If you are anything like me, you'll move super slowly, arms out in front, and shuffle your feet—all of this with the hopes that how I injure myself won't be nearly as painful as if I went full tilt. I even like to do it with my eyes closed; I know if the room is black, it doesn't make a difference, but it helps me feel like I have some semblance of control. And maybe as we begin the next step in the journey, that is how you feel too: Willing to wade around in the dark but wanting to go slow and search carefully to understand the origin story of this deep part of who you are. Please give yourself permission to go slowly, and if you find it easily—great! If it takes a little longer—no problem. Judging yourself throughout the process isn't super helpful and can sometimes keep you anchored from conscious learning.

The best place I've found to begin the search for your wound is by using something I call the emotional intensity scale. This simple but powerful tool was introduced to me by my counselor, and it has become invaluable in helping me process and understand my emotional reactions. The emotional intensity scale is essentially a way to measure how strongly you feel about a situation or experience, helping you to identify moments when you're emotionally "spiked." These spikes often point to deeper wounds that are crying out for attention.

The scale works by giving you a tool to pause and assess the level of intensity you're feeling in any given moment, assigning a number or descriptor to your emotions. For example, a mild frustration might rate as a two or three, while a full-blown emotional reaction—like anger, fear, or sadness—might feel like a nine or ten. The goal isn't to judge or suppress your emotions but to become more aware of them. When you consistently find yourself spiking at a high intensity over certain triggers, it's a clue that something deeper is at play. If you are spiked above a six it is almost always more about you than it is the other person.

What makes this tool so effective is its intentionality. Instead of letting emotions control you or bottling them up, the scale gives you a framework to explore what's beneath the surface. When something "spikes" you, it's often because it's brushing up against an unhealed wound or unresolved issue. For instance, if you find yourself overreacting to criticism at work, it might be linked to a childhood wound of feeling undervalued or overlooked. If a seemingly minor disagreement in a relationship sends you into a spiral, it could point to a fear of abandonment or rejection rooted in your formative years.

The beauty of the emotional intensity scale is that it acts like a compass, guiding you toward the source of your emotional pain. It shifts your focus from reacting to reflecting. Instead of asking, "Why is this happening to me?" you begin to ask, "Why am I responding this way?" That simple shift in perspective opens the door to deeper self-awareness and, ultimately, healing.

Using this tool requires practice and honesty. It's not always easy to sit with our emotions and trace them back to their origins, but the effort is worth it. As you learn to identify and explore these emotional spikes, you'll begin to uncover the wounds that need your attention. You'll see patterns you might have missed before and start to understand how those wounds have shaped your life. Most importantly, you'll gain clarity about where healing needs to happen and how to move forward with intention and grace. Let's take a moment to practice: Close your eyes, and remember the last time you got fired up about something. When were you above a six? What was happening? Who was around? After you've fully acknowledged what was happening in the moment, I want you to wrestle with these questions: What were the other times in your life you felt this way? When was the first time? Wrestling with questions like these is how you can wisely use the scale to dive deeper into your wound.

The scale isn't just for moments of negative emotions either. Positive emotional intensity—the times when you feel exhilarated or deeply moved—can also point to your wound. For instance, if you find yourself disproportionately elated by a piece of praise or validation, it might be worth exploring whether it's tapping into a part of you that has long craved recognition or approval. These moments, though joyful, can reveal just as much about your inner world as the more difficult ones. Let me give you some examples.

Imagine you are driving down the highway and someone cuts you off, not paying a lick of attention. If that action leads you to give that driver the "middle finger salute" or launches you into a tirade of expletives, then it is likely that you aren't just upset about the driver cutting you off. Instead, the action of being cut off has bumped up against your wound. Perhaps it's touching a deeper feeling of being disrespected or ignored, something that might stem from an experience where you felt unseen or unimportant. In that moment, it's not about the driver's mistake but about the unresolved feelings the situation has triggered within you.

Here's another example. Let's say you have a twelve-year-old daughter. When you ask her to put away the dishes, she rolls her eyes and begins to whine about how she doesn't want to. Her reaction sends you into a fifteen-minute tirade about all the things you provide for her. If this happens, it's likely she's just bumped up against your wound. Maybe her reaction made you feel unappreciated or undervalued, echoing a deeper narrative from your past. Perhaps you grew up in a household where your contributions were overlooked, or you've experienced relationships where your efforts were taken for granted. Her eyeroll and whining weren't the actual reason for your tirade; they were just the spark that ignited something far more significant inside you.

These examples demonstrate how seemingly minor interactions can provoke disproportionate reactions when they connect with our wounds. It's rarely about the other person's behavior alone. Instead, it's an invitation to reflect on what lies beneath the surface and explore the stories or experiences that shaped our emotional triggers.

It doesn't just work on bad things though; the emotional intensity scale also works on good things. For example, let's say you have a son who is a middle linebacker for the football team. During a big game, your son intercepts the ball and takes it in for a game-winning touchdown. In that moment, you, as the parent, lose your mind with excitement—high-fiving everyone around you, chest bumping, screaming at the top of your lungs. That level of emotional intensity might not just be about pride in your son's achievement. It could be that the moment bumped up against a wound tied to your own past. Maybe you grew up feeling overlooked in your athletic or personal accomplishments, and your son's success feels like a redemption of that narrative. Or perhaps you've long carried a desire for validation through external achievement, and his win becomes a surrogate for your own feelings of worth.

21

Similarly, let's say you closed a monumentally large deal at work. Instead of simply feeling proud and content, you decide to tell every person you meet, making it the center of conversation for three days straight, and even going out on a bender to celebrate. That kind of response might signal that the success tapped into something deeper. Maybe it's tied to a wound from a time when you felt undervalued in your career or personal life. The deal might feel like proof of your worth, pushing you to overemphasize the achievement in an attempt to fill a void that's been there for years.

In both examples, the heightened emotional response isn't inherently bad or may not be bad at all—it's natural to feel joy and excitement. However, the scale helps you recognize when that intensity is pointing to something more. It's an opportunity to pause and ask, "What's beneath this excitement?" Identifying these connections allows you to celebrate without being driven by unresolved wounds, giving you the freedom to experience the moment for what it truly is.

Anytime your emotional intensity spikes above a six on a scale of one to ten, it is likely that the event is bumping up against your wound. Why a six? Well, most well-adjusted adults rarely exceed a six on the emotional intensity scale. Most of the time, adults operate at a relatively low level of emotional intensity, maintaining a sense of balance and calm in their day-to-day lives. However, the emotional intensity scale isn't a one-size-fits-all tool—it's deeply personal and unique to each individual. A five for me might feel like a seven for you, and that's perfectly okay. The scale is not about comparison but self-awareness. It's not about how your emotions look *externally*; it's about how they feel *internally*. Only you can determine where you are on the scale at any given moment.

Similarly, while others might observe or comment on your emotional state, the identification of your emotions—and the wounds that might be driving them—is ultimately your responsibility. No one else can fully understand the depth or origins of what you're feeling. People can offer insight, support, and perspective, but at the end of the day, the work of self-discovery and healing is yours to do. This is a vital truth because it empowers you. It reminds you that, while you might not control the circumstances that trigger your emotions, you do control how you think, feel, and act in response to them. Owning this responsibility is key to building healthier relationships with yourself and others.

Another critical point about the emotional intensity scale is that emotional intensity isn't inherently good or bad—it simply is. Emotions are a natural part of being human, just as breathing is. God is emotional, and He gave us emotions—it is one of the ways we are made in His image. To shame yourself for feeling deeply is as unreasonable as blaming yourself for needing air. High emotional intensity doesn't mean you're broken, weak, or incapable; it means you're alive, attuned, and responsive to the world around you. The key is not to avoid emotional intensity but to understand it. Why are you at a six—or a seven or eight? What's triggering that reaction? What is this emotional spike trying to tell you about your experiences, your wounds, and your needs?

We'll dive deeper into this concept in the next chapter, but for now, it's important to release yourself from the grip of self-criticism. Your emotions are not the problem; they're the signals. They point to areas in your life that need attention, healing, or boundaries. By embracing your emotional intensity as a part of your humanity rather than resisting or suppressing it, you open the door to greater self-awareness and growth. When you can view your emotions without judgment, you create the space to explore their origins and allow healing to begin.

As you begin to become more and more aware of your emotional intensity scale, you begin to see patterns, and those patterns help outline the edges of your wound. In the examples I gave above, there are some clear wounds that form a pattern:

- Getting cut off by the driver, getting excited about the football play. Both of those examples could lead to a conclusion that you didn't feel seen as a child. You wrestle with feeling like you have a voice in the world.

- The daughter rolling her eyes, closing the big deal. These could inform us that you didn't feel like you had respect in the household growing up, and as a result, it is something you desperately crave as an adult.

Some other common wounds have to do with chaos and order, feeling like you need a sense of peace, or having trust issues. If you can begin to notice the activities that spike you emotionally, you'll begin to see the patterns.

Noticing the patterns is what I call "getting to know the edges of your wound." The funny part about the wound is that because it comes with you everywhere you go, it shows up differently in every situation. Let me give you an example. I mentioned that my wound comes from not feeling seen (again, no one's fault, no one did this to me—just part of the brokenness of the world). So, here I am trying to lead a church, and a church member comes into my office to question my integrity about financial decisions. The church member was convinced that I had done something inappropriate with the finances; I knew that I hadn't. I actually put in checks and balances to make sure that it was nearly impossible for that to happen, and yet when the accusation was made, I immediately became incensed. I was furious. I was hurt. I was all the things. The conversation wasn't productive, and when the member left my office, I immediately began to cry. Think about all that emotion, even though I knew I hadn't done anything wrong. Why did it bother me so much? Well, because the situation bumped up against my wound. The church member didn't do anything wrong; it wasn't anyone's fault. The member had a concern and addressed the concern, and I responded with intense emotions. Again, this isn't good or bad; it just is. I had an emotional reaction because it bumped up against the edge of my wound that felt like the church member didn't see my heart. Sometimes, pain like that just exists. It wasn't the church member's fault. It wasn't my fault. It was a wound neither of us could see in the moment.

After sorting through that intense emotional response, I was able to identify that it was part of my wound. In hindsight, I wish I would have been able to give myself some space before trying to process the request. In most cases, that much emotion isn't productive for solving the problem (if a problem exists). The thing about the edge of your wound and emotional intensity—they are actually two of the best indicators that someone is getting close to your pain. Find your pain, find your wound.

The edges of your wound are like sensitive boundaries that alert you when someone or something is getting close to your pain. Think of it like pressing on a bruise—it's not the surface that's injured but the deeper tissue underneath. The edges of your wound may not always feel like pain in the traditional sense; sometimes, they manifest as defensiveness, irritation, or an oversized emotional reaction to what might seem like a minor event. These edges act as emotional tripwires, signaling that there's something beneath the surface that needs attention. Paying attention to these signals is crucial because they are your body and mind's way of pointing you toward the deeper wounds inside of you. It's in these moments of heightened intensity that you have an opportunity—not to push through or ignore the feelings but to pause, reflect, and explore what's going on inside. By recognizing these edges for what they are, you can begin to navigate your emotional landscape with greater awareness and intentionality.

While pain is one way to find your wound, another way to uncover it is through your gifting. God does something truly remarkable: He takes the pain in our lives and redeems it, transforming it into something beautiful—our gift. As Romans 8:28 reminds us, *"And we know that in all things God works for the good of those who love him, who have been called according to his purpose."* This redemptive work means that on the other side of your wound, you often find your greatest gift.

When I talk about a gift, I'm not referring to physical abilities or talents like dunking a basketball, running fast, or even being incredibly attractive (which, let's be honest, you are). Instead, I'm talking about your emotional and relational gift—the unique way you show up in the world and connect with others. For example, my wounding stems from not feeling seen as a child. Out of that pain, God has given me the gift of truly seeing others at a deep, personal level. It's not always ideal for small talk, but it allows people to feel safe enough to share their hearts with me. This gift has shaped my calling, leading me to professions like pastoring and coaching where I can deeply connect with others and allow them to feel seen and valued. Through God's redemptive power, what was once a source of pain has become a source of purpose and impact.

One of the most profound ways to uncover your wounding is to reflect on your unique gifting. Often, our greatest strengths and abilities emerge from the very places where we've experienced pain, loss, or lack. These gifts are not coincidences; they are part of the redemptive work that God does in our lives, turning what once hurt us into a source of healing and purpose for ourselves and others. For example, if you excel at bringing order to chaos—sorting, organizing, and helping things or people find their rightful place—it's possible that your childhood felt disordered or chaotic. Your gift of order may have developed as a response to the instability you once experienced, giving you the ability to create calm and clarity in the midst of confusion.

Similarly, if you have a knack for disarming tense situations with humor and making people feel at ease, your gift of peace might have grown out of a childhood marked by conflict or disorder. You learned how to use humor to bridge gaps and soothe tension, and now it's a tool you wield naturally. Or perhaps you're someone who remains calm under pressure, able to bring a sense of steadiness to stressful situations. That gift of calmness may have been forged in a home where intensity was the norm, teaching you how to stay grounded amidst the storm. Even seemingly simple wounds, like feeling that your parents weren't around much because they were always working, can shape profound gifts. In this case, your wound of perceived absence may have given rise to a gift of presence. You might be someone who is unwaveringly available to those you care about, making them feel valued and supported in a way you once longed to feel yourself.

These connections between our wounds and our gifts high-light the paradoxical beauty of how we are shaped as individuals. Our gifts are not just random traits; they are deeply connected to our experiences and the ways we've learned to navigate the world. By recognizing the link between the pain we've endured and the strengths we've developed, we can begin to understand ourselves on a deeper level. This awareness allows us not only to embrace our gifts but also to address the wounds that shaped them, offer-ing the potential for even greater healing and growth. A great ex-ample of this is the story of Joseph and his brothers in the book of Genesis. Joseph experiences so much pain, and yet God redeemed those experiences. By the end of the account, Joseph is in a posi-tion that he can help the people who meant to hurt him. Genesis 50:20–21 encapsulates it perfectly: *"'You intended to harm me, but God intended it for good to accomplish what is now being done, the saving of many lives. So then, don't be afraid. I will provide for you and your children.' And he assured them and spoke kindly to them."*

I wish I could tell you that there was always a simple formula to this—that every wound fits perfectly into a category—but emo-tions don't work like that. They are nuanced and personal. God's gifts work the same way—you have been given something that is unique to you; no one else has what you have. People might have something that looks similar, but you are different, and the God of all creation has given it to you for your specific use in the world. You are equipped, you are chosen, you are called! So, as you sort out your gifting, know that it's God's way of saying, *I see your pain, and I am redeeming that pain with this incredible gift that is completely unique to you.*

Finding your wound is a lot like finding the light switch in the dark. You'll use the edges of things, the pain of situations, and certainly the gift God has given you. All of that will help you find the light switch, and here is the amazing gift: Once you find the light switch, you'll never have to be in the dark again. Do you remember the Lego metaphor? Legos aren't scary when you can see where they are—they might be annoying, but they aren't scary. Once you learn how to live with your wound, you'll know that it's there, and even on the darkest days, you won't be scared. I love what Paul writes in the book of Ephesians, chapter 5:

> *For you were once darkness, but now you are light in the Lord.*
> *Live as children of light (for the fruit of the light consists*
> *in all goodness, righteousness and truth) and find out what*
> *pleases the Lord. Have nothing to do with the fruitless deeds of*
> *darkness, but rather expose them. It is shameful even to men-*
> *tion what the disobedient do in secret. But everything exposed*
> *by the light becomes visible—and everything that is illumi-*
> *nated becomes a light. This is why it is said:*
>
> > *"Wake up, sleeper,*
> >
> > *rise from the dead,*
> >
> > *and Christ will shine on you." (8–14)*

Over the years, I've discovered a profound truth: There is a significant difference between pain and power. Pain, as awful as it is, is something we can endure. It's part of the human experience. Pain can be acknowledged, processed, and even healed over time. But when something has power over you, it's a completely differ-ent story. Power, in this context, doesn't just hurt—it controls. It dictates your thoughts, actions, and decisions, often without you realizing it. Power in the darkness suffocates, holding you captive and preventing you from moving forward.

When a wound remains hidden or unacknowledged, it wields immense power. It manipulates your behavior, influences your relationships, and creates patterns of reaction that feel unshakable. For example, an unacknowledged wound might cause you to lash out in anger when you feel criticized or withdraw emotionally when someone gets too close. These behaviors aren't simply painful; they are the result of the wound exerting control over your life.

Pain, on the other hand, is different. When you bring a wound into the light, it loses its power and becomes what it truly is: pain. Pain, though difficult, is something you can confront and work through. It's not pleasant, but it is finite—it doesn't have to dictate your actions or control your future. When you name your wound and begin to understand it, you strip it of its ability to dominate your life. You reclaim your agency and begin the journey of healing.

This distinction is crucial because it reminds us that we can live with pain, but we cannot truly live when something has power over us. Pain, when acknowledged, can become a stepping stone to growth. It can teach us, refine us, and even make us stronger. Power, on the other hand, traps us in a cycle of fear, avoidance, and reaction, leaving us stuck in the shadows of our wounds. Another way to think about it is like this: Pain is a storm. It's scary, it hurts, and you aren't sure what life is going to be like on the other side. When something has power over you, it isn't a storm–it's a prison. It's much more difficult to have hope, to see the other side, and to believe that there is even a way out. Pain is manageable, but when something has power over you, it can suffocate you down to the soul.

Acknowledging this difference is the first step toward freedom. It's the moment you decide to bring your wounds into the light, to face the pain, and to break free from the power they've held over you. The journey may not be easy, but it's one of the most liberating and life-giving things you can do. Here's to taking those first courageous steps and may your path toward uncovering your wounds and reclaiming your power be filled with grace and hope.

The Wound Identification Guide

Step 1: Recognizing Emotional Intensity (The Emotional Intensity Scale)

- Reflect on situations where your emotions spike above a **six out of ten.** It is important to have more than one data point so you can begin to look for patterns.
- Write down moments when you felt an unusually strong emotional reaction (anger, sadness, defensiveness, overwhelming joy, or deep validation).
- Ask yourself about each situation:
    - What was happening at that moment?
    - What specific words or actions triggered the reaction?
    - Was it something that has happened before?

Step 2: Patterns in Emotional Triggers

- Identify recurring themes in your emotional responses.
- Do you notice a **common thread** in the situations that trigger a strong reaction? (e.g., feeling unseen, not being heard, rejection, failure, control)
- Circle the themes that show up the most.

Step 3: Looking Back at Childhood & Early Influences

- Wounds often form between **ages 4–12**.
- Think about your childhood experiences:
  - What were moments where you felt hurt, misunderstood, or abandoned?
  - Were there recurring messages you received from parents, teachers, or peers? (e.g., "You're not good enough," "You have to be perfect," "Your needs aren't important?"

Step 4: Connecting the Dots

- Compare your **emotional intensity spikes** with your **childhood messages** and see if there is alignment.
- How do those childhood wounds still show up in your current relationships, leadership, or parenting?
- What core belief might have formed as a result of that wound? (e.g., "I have to prove myself to be valuable," "If I open up to people in my life, I will eventually be rejected by those people.")

Step 5: Naming the Wound

- Write down a **one-sentence** description of your wound:
  - Example: "I fear being unworthy unless I achieve."
  - Example: "I feel like I am only valued when I am needed."

Step 6: Reflect on How It Shapes Your Life

- How does this wound show up in your daily decisions?
- Does it affect your leadership, parenting, or relationships?
- When do you notice it the most?

I know it can be difficult to sort out what your wound is, so here are five common examples of wounding and how they show up:

1. Rejection Wound (*Feeling Unwanted or Unworthy*)

- **Example:** A child who felt dismissed by a parent, teacher, or peer group may grow up believing they are not enough or that love must be earned.
- **How It Shows Up:** Fear of abandonment, people-pleasing, avoiding vulnerability, or difficulty forming deep relationships.
- **Trigger Example:** Feeling ignored or not invited to an event might trigger deep feelings of being unworthy.

2. Abandonment Wound (*Feeling Alone or Unprotected*)

- **Example:** A child whose parent was emotionally or physically absent may struggle with feeling secure in relationships.
- **How It Shows Up:** Fear of being left, anxiety in relationships, over-attachment, or difficulty trusting others.
- **Trigger Example:** A spouse or friend not responding to a text quickly may create panic and insecurity.

3. Betrayal Wound (*Feeling Deceived or Let Down by Someone You Trusted*)

- **Example:** Experiencing dishonesty, broken promises, or unfaithfulness from a loved one creates trust issues.
- **How It Shows Up:** Control issues, hypervigilance, suspicion, or difficulty relying on others.
- **Trigger Example:** A co-worker taking credit for your idea could ignite past betrayal wounds.

4. Humiliation Wound (*Feeling Ashamed or Not Good Enough*)

- **Example:** A child who was frequently criticized, laughed at, or shamed may grow up feeling like they are defective.

- **How It Shows Up:** Perfectionism, defensiveness, self-sabotage, or a need for validation.

- **Trigger Example:** Making a minor mistake at work and feeling overwhelmingly embarrassed, as if it defines your worth.

5. Injustice Wound (*Feeling That Life Is Unfair or That You Must Prove Yourself*)

- **Example:** A child who was raised in a highly strict or overly critical environment may feel like they always have to fight to be heard or respected.

- **How It Shows Up:** Rigid thinking, anger, difficulty accepting grace, or excessive self-discipline.

- **Trigger Example:** A supervisor correcting your work may feel like an attack on your competence, even if it's constructive criticism.

Exercise:

1. **Journaling Prompt:** Write down moments when you've felt particularly emotional. What were the circumstances, and how did you react?

2. **Emotional Awareness:** What recurring themes or feelings might point to a deeper wound?

3. **Challenge:** Take the time to talk to your inner circle about the wound and the greatest gift. Ask them what they see inside of you and if they agree with your analysis of gifting/wound. Remember, we aren't going to them for approval, but we are asking them if they see what we see.

Chapter 3

Feel Your Feelings

When Jesus saw her weeping, and the Jews who had come along with her also weeping, he was deeply moved in spirit and troubled. "Where have you laid him?" he asked. "Come and see, Lord," they replied. Jesus wept. Then the Jews said, "See how he loved him!"

– John 11:33–36

"You just have to sit in it." When my counselor first told me this, I felt an overwhelming sense of frustration and confusion. Sit in it? I didn't even know what that meant. How do you sit in something so abstract, so intangible? It felt like being handed a task with no instructions, no roadmap. At the time, I was desperate for a solution—I wanted to fix the problem, solve for X, and move on with my life. I didn't want to feel these emotions, let alone sit with them. I wanted them to go away, to disappear, so I could get back to my routine and regain some semblance of control.

But every time I brought this frustration to my counselor, his response was the same, calm, unwavering, and maddeningly consistent: "You have to sit in your feelings." No shortcuts. No quick fixes. Just sit with them. To me, it felt like the emotional equivalent of standing in a burning building and being told not to run. I wanted action, a plan to extinguish the flames. Instead, I was being asked to stop, to feel the heat, and to notice what was happening around me and within me.

What I eventually realized was that my counselor wasn't trying to frustrate me—he was trying to teach me something profound about emotions. Emotions aren't problems to be solved; they're signals to be understood. When we try to push them away or numb them, we miss the message they're trying to deliver. Sitting in it doesn't mean wallowing in despair or giving up on finding solutions. It means creating space to acknowledge and explore what's festering beneath the surface. It's about letting yourself feel without judgment, letting yourself process without rushing to fix.

This practice of "sitting in it" is uncomfortable, especially for someone like me who thrives on solving problems and moving forward. But I learned (and I'm still learning) that by avoiding my emotions, I was actually giving them more power. The feelings I tried to suppress didn't disappear—they festered, manifesting in other ways and pulling me further from the peace I was seeking. Sitting with them, as hard as it was, allowed me to name them, understand them, and eventually release them.

Ten years of counseling and it finally became more and more clear to me. Feelings are just meant to be felt; they aren't there to dictate action, and they certainly aren't meant to control our life. Feelings are decision-*points* not decision-*makers*. So, the best thing that we can do to honor our feelings is to actually give them space, to acknowledge their presence in our lives, and to say, "I see you." Emotions are a hallmark of humanity and a gift from God. Jesus was highly emotional yet never emotionally led. Instead, Jesus was led by the Father, through the power of the Holy Spirit and was still very emotional. It's one of the things that I appreciate most about the story where Jesus raises Lazurus from the dead. It is an emotional story.

Take a look at Jesus in John's gospel:

When Jesus saw her weeping, and the Jews who had come along with her also weeping, he was deeply moved in spirit and troubled. "Where have you laid him?" he asked.

"Come and see, Lord," they replied.

Jesus wept.

Then the Jews said, "See how he loved him!"

But some of them said, "Could not he who opened the eyes of the blind man have kept this man from dying?"

Jesus, once more deeply moved, came to the tomb. It was a cave with a stone laid across the entrance. "Take away the stone," he said.

"But, Lord," said Martha, the sister of the dead man, "by this time there is a bad odor, for he has been there four days."

Then Jesus said, "Did I not tell you that if you believe, you will see the glory of God?"

So they took away the stone. Then Jesus looked up and said, "Father, I thank you that you have heard me. I knew that you always hear me, but I said this for the benefit of the people standing here, that they may believe that you sent me."

When he had said this, Jesus called in a loud voice, "Lazarus, come out!" The dead man came out, his hands and feet wrapped with strips of linen, and a cloth around his face.

Jesus said to them, "Take off the grave clothes and let him go."

John 11:3–44

The emotion in this story is deep and beautiful; Jesus wept, and Jesus was deeply moved. Jesus felt all the feelings and still was grateful and obedient to the Father. Jesus was emotional yet stayed the course of obedience with the Father. And he stayed on mission for what the Father was calling Him to be during His time on Earth. One of the things I've observed when working with leaders is how often emotional reactions take the reins and change the course of their decisions and actions. In moments of heightened emotional intensity—whether it's frustration, fear, anger, or even excitement—it's easy to let emotions dictate what comes next. Instead of pausing to process or reflect, we react impulsively, and before we know it, we're a puddle of emotion, overwhelmed and without clarity. In these moments, the ability to lead effectively diminishes because we're no longer operating from a place of intentionality but from raw, unchecked emotions.

Even more damaging, though, is the other extreme: reacting out of emotion without thoughtful consideration. In this scenario, instead of pausing to regain composure or evaluate the situation, we let the emotional spike drive us forward. We charge ahead without a strategic or measured response, and all too often, the result is relational brokenness. A harsh word spoken in frustration, a rash decision made in fear, or a defensive move made out of insecurity can leave a wake of damaged relationships, lost trust, and regret. As leaders, the cleanup from these moments can be exhausting and demoralizing, especially when we recognize that much of it could have been avoided with a little more self-awareness and self-regulation.

What's critical to understand is that emotions themselves are not the enemy. Emotions are essential—they give us insight into what we care about, what we fear, and what's important to us.

The problem arises when we allow those emotions to control our actions without filtering them through wisdom, perspective, and the broader context of our mission and values. Leadership requires us to *acknowledge our emotions without being ruled by them.* It requires us to balance emotional honesty with thoughtful restraint.

This isn't easy, especially in high-pressure situations where emotions naturally run high, but it's in these moments that leaders are tested. The ability to pause, reflect, and choose a response rather than reacting impulsively is what separates emotionally intelligent leaders from those who leave relational wreckage in their wake. As Proverbs 29:11 reminds us, *"Fools give full vent to their rage, but the wise bring calm in the end."* Wise leadership isn't about suppressing emotions; it's about managing them well.

When leaders develop the discipline to navigate their emotions effectively, they gain clarity and create space for thoughtful, strategic responses. They cultivate trust in their teams because their actions are consistent and intentional, not reactive or erratic. And most importantly, they model a way of leading that values relationships as much as results, understanding that emotional self-regulation is key to fostering both healthy teams and lasting impact.

This is why sitting in our feelings is so essential. When we're brave enough to sit with our emotions instead of reacting to them, we gain the clarity and perspective needed to avoid letting those emotions make decisions for us—decisions that could lead to unintended and often painful consequences. Sitting in our feelings creates a pause, a moment to breathe and reflect, instead of rushing headlong into action driven by the intensity of the moment. It's not about ignoring or suppressing your feelings but about honoring them as messengers without allowing them to dictate your course.

So why talk about sitting in our feelings in a book that's all about finding your wound? Because one of the most effective ways to uncover your wound is by listening to your feelings. Our emotions are like signposts, pointing us toward the deeper parts of ourselves that need attention and healing. When we give space for our feelings to surface and be experienced in our everyday lives, we start to notice patterns. We see how certain interactions, situations, or words evoke strong, sometimes overwhelming, emotional responses. These responses aren't random; they're often connected to the wounds we carry.

When someone bumps up against your wound—whether intentionally or not—it's natural to feel a surge of emotion. These feelings might be anger, sadness, defensiveness, or fear, and they often feel intense, even disproportionate to the situation at hand. That's because they're not just about the present moment—they're tied to past pain that hasn't been fully processed or healed. Sitting with these feelings, as uncomfortable as it may be, is one of the greatest gifts you can give yourself. It allows you to explore the roots of your emotions, to ask, "Why am I feeling this way? What is this reaction trying to tell me about myself?"

Learning to sit in your feelings is not about wallowing in them; it's about using them as a tool for self-discovery. It's about becoming intimate with your wound and understanding its edges, its triggers, and its impact on your life. This process requires courage and patience, but it also leads to freedom. As you sit with your feelings and listen to what they're telling you, you begin to reclaim the parts of yourself that have been overshadowed by pain. You start to see your wound not just as a source of suffering but as an invitation to growth and healing. When you can identify that you are emotionally spiked above a six, you can begin the process of lowering the emotional temperature of the room. Wisdom is awareness.

This practice is deeply transformative. It helps you shift from being reactive to reflective, from feeling powerless to feeling empowered. Ultimately, it brings you closer to the truth of who you are—someone created with purpose, resilience, and the capacity to heal. Sitting with your feelings is the bridge between acknowledging your wound and beginning the journey of redemption and restoration. It's not easy, but it's worth it.

Allow me to give you an example of what this might look like in your everyday life. I was leading a small to medium-sized nonprofit, and one of the members of my community struggled with my leadership choices. Okay, I'm drastically under-selling that; I'm pretty sure this person hated me. It's okay, I know it wasn't personal, just an extreme disbelief in the vision I had for the organization, the approach I took to leading through that vision, and where I was leading the organization. Again, perfectly okay and within that person's right. However, every time that person came into my office to talk to me, it felt like a personal attack. It felt like he was dropping napalm on my heart. It bumped up against my wound every single time. In numerous conversations with my counselor, one of the suggestions was to schedule time after the meeting was over so that I could just experience the feelings. Steve, my counselor, even suggested that I curl up in a ball underneath my desk and just sit in it. While I didn't take Steve's suggestion literally, I did create space to experience my feelings after the meeting was over. I began creating buffers for emotional experiences after those meetings ended, and as a result, I didn't make rash decisions, and I didn't talk to anyone about what I was feeling until the intensity of the feelings calmed down. Said another way, I didn't share what was on my heart until my heart felt safe to share again. The practice of creating space for emotions has become an important part of managing my calendar.

One of the inescapable realities of leadership is that you will face opposition. People will challenge you, resist change, question your decisions, and push back against the status quo. At the same time, others will support you, encourage you, and even rally around your vision with enthusiasm. Both the challenges and the support evoke emotions, sometimes deeply intense emotions, that can influence how you lead. Leadership, by its very nature, is an emotional journey. The pressure, the expectations, the successes, and the setbacks all come with feelings that must be navigated thoughtfully.

At this point in the book, you might be asking yourself the question, "Is this a leadership book?" And the answer is yes but not in the traditional sense. Pastor Dave Holmes (my lead pastor) describes leadership as "the ability to exert influence." So, if you have the ability to influence anyone, you are a leader. If you have children, you lead them. If you have co-workers, you can lead them. If you have a social media platform with at least one follower, you can lead them. Leadership is influence, and in the world we live in today, we all have some influence. Don't let the word scare you; as you gain understanding of your wound, your ability to feel comfortable as a wounded leader will only continue to grow!

The wisest leaders are not those who suppress or ignore their emotions, but those who learn to experience and process them in healthy and safe surroundings. A lack of emotion isn't the hallmark of great leadership; great leadership is the ability to channel those emotions in a way that keeps you focused on the mission. Emotions, when left unchecked, can derail even the most capable leader. A sharp comment born of frustration can destroy trust. A reactive decision made in fear can undermine long-term goals. On the flip side, emotions processed in a healthy way can fuel resilience, foster empathy, and strengthen commitment.

Also, to be clear, this isn't just for organizational leaders, this is for your family too (anywhere you have influence). If you are raising kids, then you know exactly what it means to have an emotional response. I wish I could tell you that raising my three kids has been all sunshine and lollipops. My kids are great, but the truth is nothing spikes an emotional response for me more than my children. And listen, I know they're not doing it on purpose, but they are emotional humans, and I am certainly an emotional human, so when our emotions bump up against each other, they need to be felt. Part of the reason why it's so easy for our kids to spike an emotional response is because they have direct access to your heart. Same with your spouse. The more intimate a person is in your life, and the more you feel connected to them, the more it will hurt when we perceive that they are doing something "against" us.

Have you ever listened to yourself talk to your spouse on the phone? When a client calls me, I sound like the perfect gentleman: "Hello, this is Tony, how can I help you?" When my wife calls, I sound like the drive-thru worker at Taco Bell at 1am: "Hey, what do you want?!" It's probably not that extreme, but you get the idea. Familiarity breeds a lack of intentionality when it comes to family, and family is always going to be closer than other people in your life. Emotional responses matter when you lead your family.

A prime example of this is sports. We are a sporty family. We love to play all the sports… football, baseball, basketball, and cheer. Every weekend you can find us at a sports field. My middle son is especially competitive; he's passionate like his dad and aggressive and hates losing. I think he hates to lose more than he wants to win. Recently, he was playing baseball and had a play at home plate. The umpire didn't like the way that he approached home plate (he thought he should have slid), and he was ejected from the game. It was a super emotional moment, and I wasn't there to see it or to fully understand what was going on. So, on our phone call post-game, he was explaining to me what happened, and as I was preparing to give a response on what he could do better next time—he hung up on me. I was instantly above a six on the emotional intensity scale. I was furious. So, when I got him back on the phone I read him the riot act, right before his next game—not an ideal parenting moment. Once the second game was over for the day and we had an opportunity to feel our feelings, we got back on the phone, and I apologized. He apologized as well, and we acknowledged the brokenness of the moment. I'm thankful that my 14-year-old son knows that he's emotional and that emotions just need to be felt.

This is also an important lesson for leaders: if emotion does damage to a relationship, then intentional emotion should add to the healing. The process of healing emotional damage most often requires an emotional approach. If I use my words and do emotional damage to a friend, giving them a twenty-dollar bill without saying anything likely will not heal the relational divide.

Instead, it requires words and an intentional approach to close the gap in the friendship.

As you begin to become familiar with your feelings, as you feel your feelings, it is important to know this—you are going to experience feelings that may be new. A great example of this is the feeling of grief. Most people never know when grief will arrive, and most people don't know what grief will look like, and all of that can be very scary. It's scary because it's overwhelming, and it's like looking in the mirror and seeing something you've never seen before. One of the things I've noticed over the years is that when we are scared, we have a tendency to make quick decisions. Again, I just want to reiterate, the only way to experience the depth of a feeling like grief is to sit in it. We must acknowledge the feeling. That could look like journaling or talking to a friend. It could just be sitting outside in the sun and talking to God about the depth of your emotions. All these things help us deal with feelings. If you become frightened by feelings you're unfamiliar with, then please let me encourage you to reach out to someone for help. Talk to someone who's been on this journey before you and just share it out loud, letting some of the pressure release from your heart. Feelings are meant to be felt; they are decision points and not decision makers. If you don't deal with your feelings, then eventually your feelings will deal with you.

Exercise:

1. **Journaling Prompt:** Set aside ten minutes daily to sit in your feelings without judgment. Write down what comes up.

2. **Emotional Awareness:** Read John 11:33–36 and meditate on Jesus' emotional response. How does this model help you relate to your own feelings?

3. **Challenge:** Create a plan on how you can emotionally feel your feelings as a family. Maybe your family is just you and friends, maybe it's a spouse and kids—whoever you call family, tell them how you want to be intentional in emotionally feeling your feelings.

Making Good Decisions

Get wisdom, get understanding; do not forget my words or
turn away from them.

– Proverbs 4:5

We all have coping mechanisms—some good, some bad. Make no mistake, whether or not you realize it, you have ways of dealing with stress, pain, and uncertainty. Most leaders understand this truth on a surface level, but where we often fall short is in recognizing exactly what those coping mechanisms are. And where we fall even shorter is in understanding whether we are using them intentionally or simply reacting to our circumstances.

It wasn't until I stopped drinking that I fully grasped the extent of my own coping struggles. At the time, I was on staff at a great church doing meaningful work that I believed was for the Lord. I took pride in that work—righteous pride, or so I thought. But that pride, which I was so eager to share, slowly became a disruption in my family life. My leadership and my faith were strong, yet something wasn't right.

During that season, I was promoted to oversee the recovery community at the church. Becoming part of that community was a game-changer. I was surrounded by some of the most incredible people I'd ever met, and my leadership team pushed me to grow beyond where I was. They challenged me to stop drinking. At first, I resisted, believing my drinking wasn't an issue. But as I stepped into sobriety, I had a realization: I didn't have a drinking problem—I had a coping problem. I struggled to cope. I struggled to navigate my emotions in a healthy way. I struggled to make the right choices at the right time when faced with overwhelming feelings. My drinking wasn't the issue—it was merely a symptom of a deeper struggle to handle life's pressures in a constructive way. That revelation changed everything.

When I stopped drinking, I immediately turned to food. I still turn to food as a coping mechanism. When I'm happy, I eat. When I'm sad, I eat. I love to eat... LOL. However, I quickly realized that this wasn't a great way to cope with my pain either. So, I stopped eating, and I turned to sugar—which was equally as destructive to my body as the large amounts of food I had been eating. The sugar intake was also a problem. So, then, I began to go to the gym and work out in general. That was a much healthier coping mechanism, but since I didn't fully comprehend that I was coping at the time, it didn't dull the pain from the edge that I wish it would have. I think that's an important lesson for all of us leaders: The lack of intentionality around *why* we're doing something can greatly reduce the benefits of doing it. When we are clear about why we were there doing what we were doing *and* the purpose of the activity, it can be a catalyst to healing in many ways.

Today through lots of work and intentional choices, I know what my coping mechanisms are. Sometimes, when I'm stressed out about clients or work, I like to apply for jobs that I'm not qualified for and write ridiculous cover letters just to see if I get a response. It clearly serves that goal for me of feeling wanted or seen, and even though I've never taken one of those jobs, it always makes me feel a little bit better. I've also learned that I must be intentional about how I share that with my wife because while it's *my* coping mechanism, all it does is stress her out! She doesn't like the feeling of instability, but for me, the instability feels good. Like I have options or choices. The best part about it is that I know it's a coping mechanism, so I don't have to let it dictate my future.

Let me be clear about something that I now know I didn't have a full grasp of in that painful season of my life: Jesus is the best coping mechanism. Praying with Jesus, spending time with Jesus, and reading God's word all go a long way toward helping you cope.

Understanding our coping mechanisms is a vital step in uncovering and addressing our wounds. Coping mechanisms are the strategies—both conscious and unconscious—that we use to navigate pain, fear, or discomfort. They are our mind and body's way of protecting us from the emotional intensity of life's challenges. While these mechanisms often serve a purpose in the moment, they can also act as clues pointing us toward the underlying wounds we may not have fully acknowledged.

When we take time to reflect on *why* we cope in certain ways, we begin to recognize patterns that reveal deeper truths about ourselves. For instance, if you tend to withdraw when conflict arises, it might be because conflict bumps up against a fear of rejection or criticism rooted in a past wound. If you find yourself constantly striving for perfection, it could be a response to feeling like you were never "enough" growing up. Coping mechanisms are like signposts, guiding us toward the areas of our lives where we've felt hurt, frustration, or fear.

By understanding our coping mechanisms, we gain insight into how we respond when someone or something bumps up against parts of ourselves that we'd rather avoid—those areas of frustration, fear, or discomfort that trigger emotional intensity. These triggers often aren't random; they're connected to the parts of our identity that have been shaped by our wounds. When we cope, we're not just reacting to the present moment; we're responding to the echoes of past experiences that have left a mark on us.

This self-awareness is powerful. Recognizing your coping mechanisms gives you the wisdom to pause and ask. *What is this reaction telling me about myself? Where is this coming from? Does this activity bring me closer to Jesus?* Instead of being controlled by automatic responses, you begin to approach them with curiosity and compassion. You start to see coping mechanisms not as failures or flaws but as indicators of where healing is needed. They help you locate the edges of your wound and understand the emotional intensity that arises in certain situations.

Ultimately, understanding your coping mechanisms equips you to navigate life with greater intentionality. It allows you to choose healthier ways of responding to emotional intensity and to address the wounds that lie beneath your reactions. As Proverbs 4:7 says, *"The beginning of wisdom is this: Get wisdom. Though it cost all you have, get understanding."* Knowing why you cope the way you do is the beginning of that understanding. It's the first step toward breaking free from unhealthy patterns, embracing your true self, and finding healing for the wounds that have shaped you.

Once you've identified the wound, the process of learning its edges is what I call "diving into the wound." Diving into the wound is the deep work of learning the edges and knowing when someone bumps up against it. We already talked about the emotional intensity scale, and I do believe that is your best tool for identifying when something has got you fired up. However, over time, you'll begin to realize that there are many other facets to the depth of your wound. This is why it's important to give yourself space for emotional recognition of moments that feel intense. It's also why it's important to think about the wound as more of a lens through which you see the world, rather than an event that happened.

Actually, the imagery that I like the best is to think about the wound as an oddly shaped amoeba on my chest (as I mentioned in Chapter 1). My heart is in the middle, but all around it is the wound. The wound isn't clearly shaped, it is not very defined, and it can shift from time to time, but in order to get to my heart, you have to wade through the wound. You have to be willing to deal with my emotional intensity and my need to be seen in order to get all of me. This is also why marriage is challenging because it's two wounded people just bumping up against each other's wounds every single day. It's a process of learning the hurt of the person you care for the most and then spending an entire lifetime not stepping in it and apologizing when you do. It's also helping your spouse become familiar and intimate with their wound so they don't have to be scared of their pain. Lifelong relationships benefit from taking the time to do the wound work together.

Eventually, in every relationship and in every place where you show up, so will your wound.

Making good decisions starts with self-awareness: understanding the edges of your wound and recognizing when something is bumping against them. When we know the boundaries of our emotional pain, we can better identify when our reactions are driven by our wounds rather than by wisdom. This awareness, combined with an understanding of our coping mechanisms, gives us clarity about how and why we respond the way we do in challenging situations.

The goal isn't to stop you from having coping mechanisms. Coping mechanisms serve a purpose—they are ways we protect ourselves and navigate life's difficulties. Instead, the aim is to develop awareness. When you understand your coping strategies, you can ask yourself critical questions in the decision-making process: *Am I responding to the current situation, or am I reacting to something deeper within me? Is this decision aligned with my values and mission, or is it being driven by fear, frustration, or insecurity?*

Feelings are a crucial part of this process, but they are not decision-makers—they are decision points. Emotions serve as signals, alerting us to areas that need attention, but they should not dictate our actions. For example, anger might signal that a boundary has been crossed, but it doesn't mean the best decision is to lash out. Fear might warn you of potential danger, but it doesn't mean avoidance is the right response. The key is to pause, acknowledge what you're feeling, and then engage your deeper sense of purpose and clarity before acting.

The heart of making good decisions is being crystal clear on your "why." Your "why" is also a catalyst for not choosing something. Being clear on your "why" can be an incredible catalyst to a life that is not passive but rather intentional in all the decisions you choose to make (even if that decision is just being still!). This means understanding not only what you are choosing but also why you are choosing it. It's about aligning your decisions with your core values, your mission, and the person you want to become. It's about having a deep appreciation for what got you to this moment in the first place—the experiences, challenges, and lessons that have shaped you. When you have clarity about your why, you can make decisions that are intentional and impactful, rather than reactive and shortsighted.

Ultimately, good decision making is a process of balancing awareness and intentionality. Knowing the edges of your wound + Knowing your coping mechanisms = Knowing if you are being wise or being reactive. Wisdom comes when you recognize the triggers that might lead you astray and consciously choose a path that aligns with your values and long-term goals. It's not about avoiding feelings but about stewarding them well so that they inform your decisions rather than control them. In this way, you not only make better decisions, but you also grow as a person and a leader, fostering greater alignment between your actions and your purpose.

I recently had the opportunity to take my family to New York City. It was an incredible trip. Being from the Midwest, I don't have much experience with mass transit. We don't have any subways in Dayton, Ohio. So, as we were traversing the city, we relied heavily on Google Maps. Did you know you can put a destination into Google Maps, and it will help you navigate the transit system down to the minute? It is truly amazing. And for my little family in this big city, it was nothing short of miraculous. Now, here is the thing they don't tell you in the tourist brochure about Google

Maps. You had better be sure about where you are before you start using it to traipse around the city. Sometimes, it is hard for the GPS to work properly because everything you are doing is bouncing off of the buildings around you. Next thing you know, you've walked seven blocks in the wrong direction because you thought you were going north when you were actually going south. And to be clear, there is not much worse than leading your tired, hungry, and exhausted family in the wrong direction for seven blocks.

The same thing is true for making good decisions in your own life. You need to have a ground zero; you need to understand the starting point and be clear about exactly where you are. Good, bad, right, wrong—they are all subjective if you don't know where you are. If you aren't rooted in some sort of truth about who or where you are, it is quite possible that the journey of self-awareness around your wound, or learning the edges of your wound, can throw you to a place you don't want to be. Take the time to understand your current position, what you are doing, and how you are going to get from where you are to where God is calling you next.

When you become truly clear about your coping mechanisms, when you learn the edges of your wound, and when you gain a full understanding of where you are emotionally and spiritually, a remarkable transformation begins to take place: Your wound loses its power to dictate the outcomes in your life. It doesn't mean that the wound disappears or the pain magically vanishes, but it does mean the wound no longer gets to call the shots.

In many ways, it's like moving the wound from the driver's seat to the passenger's seat. For too long, the wound may have been in control, steering your reactions, shaping your decisions, and influencing your relationships in ways you didn't even realize.

The wound in our life has its foot on the brake and the gas, often dictating if we are moving forward or standing still. But when you bring awareness and intentionality into the process, you take back the wheel. Moving the wound to the passenger's seat changes everything—it shifts your perspective and allows you to see the road ahead more clearly. It gives you the ability to choose your path rather than being unconsciously driven by pain, fear, or insecurity.

This shift gives you something even more powerful: your voice. The voice that may have been drowned out by the noise of self-doubt, shame, or unprocessed emotions begins to emerge with strength and clarity. When the wound is no longer in charge, you're able to respond to life's challenges from a place of wisdom and alignment rather than reactivity. You regain the control you need to live out the calling God has placed on your life. As Isaiah 30:21 reminds us, "*Whether you turn to the right or to the left, your ears will hear a voice behind you, saying, 'This is the way; walk in it.'*"

By reclaiming your voice, you can engage with your life and your relationships with greater authenticity and purpose. You're no longer bound by the old patterns and narratives that the wound used to impose on you. Instead, you are free to live with intentionality, fully stepping into the person God created you to be. This process doesn't just change your perspective—it changes your trajectory, allowing you to move forward with confidence, peace, and the assurance that, while the wound may still be part of your story, it no longer gets to write the ending.

Exercise:

1. **Journaling Prompt:** List your coping mechanisms. Which ones are healthy, and which might need adjustment?

2. **Emotional Awareness:** The next time you feel intense emotions, pause and reflect before making a decision. Write down the outcome.

3. **Challenge:** Talk to someone you trust about whether or not you've been letting your wound drive you around. Create a plan to move it to the passenger seat.

Love Your Wound, Find Your Gift

In him we have redemption through his blood, the forgiveness
of sins, in accordance with the riches of God's grace.

– Ephesians 1:7

Let me share a little-discussed fact about parenting: There will come a day when you look at your child and realize that you are, in many ways, parenting yourself. It was a sobering and humbling moment. For me, this realization hit hard when my oldest child turned 16. As I watched him navigate life, I saw so many of my own traits reflected in him—his fierce independence, his resistance to being told what to do, and his reluctance to discuss decisions, especially if those decisions might threaten the freedom he valued so deeply. It was like staring into a mirror that reflected both the best and most challenging parts of myself.

At that point, it became clear that our usual approach to parenting wasn't going to work if we wanted to maintain a healthy relationship moving forward. We had to rethink our strategy. This realization led to what we called "Amnesty Dinners." These dinners weren't just meals; they were intentional spaces of grace. The idea was simple but profound: take him out to dinner, create a safe and neutral environment, and give him the freedom to say anything—about his life, his choices, or even his frustrations with us—without fear of punishment or backlash.

Amnesty Dinners were our way of bridging the relational gap. They were an attempt to prioritize the relationship over the rules, to extend grace in a way that fostered trust and openness. And what's remarkable is that they worked. Sitting across from each other in that space of mutual respect, we had the hard conversations we might never have had otherwise. He opened up, not because he had to but because he felt safe to do so. The absence of fear allowed honesty to flourish.

What struck me most about these dinners was how they mirrored God's approach to grace in our lives. Just as we offered our child a space free of fear and punishment, God invites us to come as we are, to bring our burdens, our mistakes, and even our defiance, and lay them before Him without condemnation. As Romans 8:1 says, *"Therefore, there is now no condemnation for those who are in Christ Jesus."* That grace creates space for transformation—not through force but through love.

I want to give you permission, right here and right now—you aren't going to get in trouble for your wound. Whatever fear of punishment you've been holding onto, whether it's a fear of rejection, judgment, or even eternal consequences, you can let that go. Your wound is not a moral failing or a reason for condemnation. It's part of your story and part of your humanity. Just like at the Amnesty Dinners where the fear of punishment was removed to create a safe space for honesty, I want you to approach your wound with the same grace. When the fear of punishment is gone, what remains is freedom—the freedom to acknowledge, explore, and even embrace the messy beauty of who you are.

Your wound is a beautiful, messy part of you. It's not something to hide in shame or dismiss as unworthy. In many ways, it's like the art you get from a toddler—scribbles and smudges that might not make much sense to anyone else, but to you, it's priceless. You'd put it in a frame, show it off to friends, and cherish it, not because it's perfect but because it's real, and it represents something meaningful. Your wound is similar—it might feel chaotic, hard to define, and even a little confusing, but it's a vital part of your story. It's shaped you in ways that have made you who you are, and the world is better for it.

Fear of punishment often keeps us from looking at our wounds with this kind of perspective. We worry that acknowledging them will lead to shame or that others might see us as broken or weak. But the truth is, your wound is not a mark against you; it's a testament to your resilience. It's a part of your unique, God-given identity. Just as we extended grace to our child during the Amnesty Dinners, God extends grace to us in ways that are far greater. His invitation is clear: There is no condemnation, only love and an open space to bring all of yourself, including your wounds. As 1 John 4:18 reminds us, *"There is no fear in love. But perfect love drives out fear, because fear has to do with punishment."*

When you release the fear of punishment, you can start giving your wound the attention it deserves—not as something to be fixed or erased but as something to be understood, loved, and even celebrated. Your wound is a critical part of your existence, and when you stop fighting it and start embracing it, you'll begin to see how it has helped shape the person you've become. And let me tell you, we all think that person is pretty great! Your wound isn't a liability; it's a part of your humanity, your story, and even your gift to the world.

At this point in the book, you likely have a sense of what your wound is. You might not be on a first-name basis with it just yet, but you probably have a general idea of its nature and where it originated. In other words, you've started to notice when it shows up. This awareness is a significant step forward because recognizing your wound in action is the foundation for understanding it. Remember the emotional intensity scale? It's a fantastic tool for identifying when something is bumping up against your wound. Those moments of heightened intensity—when you feel sensitive, raw, or emotionally charged—are signals that your wound is being touched. It's in these moments that we face a crucial choice about how to respond.

Here's the thing: Most of us don't respond to our wounds in the healthiest way. Instead, we tend to judge them. Judging our wounds is a natural reaction—it's what many of us have been conditioned to do. But while it's normal, it's not helpful. Judgment often brings its unwelcome companions: guilt and shame. These feelings are also incredibly common, but they don't lead to healing. In fact, they often pull us further away from understanding and embracing our wound. If you're anything like me, when something bumps up against your wound, there's this almost automatic tendency to try to "fix" it by willing yourself to be better, stronger, or less affected. It's as though we think we can talk ourselves out of the pain. Here's a great example:

I randomly happened to get into a conversation with a podcast host that I deeply respect. He is one of the people who I try to emulate regularly; I just have so much respect for his work. As were in the conversation, I just kept talking. It was like one of those moments where I could see the words leaving my mouth, and there was nothing I could do to stop it. There was no regular rhythm to the conversation; I turned it into a full blown "brag session" about all the things I was doing. I wanted to impress this particular podcaster so badly I lost all sense of EQ and made the entire conversation about me. Remember my wound: I want to be seen! So, in an effort to be seen by this particular individual, I ended up with diarrhea of the mouth. As you can imagine, I left the conversation feeling embarrassed and convinced that this person—who I wanted to impress—now thinks I am a self-absorbed egomaniac. Is that true? Of course not. Does that person think that about me? I have no way of knowing for sure, but chances are good the answer is no. Did I leave that conversation in a worse place than when I started? You betcha.

And that is how judgment, guilt, and shame can so quickly overtake our thought processes. It sneaks up on us, catching us off guard, and before we know it, a single moment—a conversation, a misunderstanding, a small misstep—has the power to shape the rest of our day. The scary part is how seamlessly it happens. That one interaction can linger in our minds, replaying on a loop, coloring every subsequent experience with a shade of self-doubt or regret. It's easy to let those feelings fester, to let them define how we see ourselves in that moment, but here's the challenge: Instead of letting judgment, guilt, and shame take over, we have to learn to respond with grace, humor, and love toward our wound.

Learning to laugh at your wound might sound counterintuitive, but it's one of the most liberating things you can do. It doesn't mean dismissing the wound or pretending it doesn't matter. It means shifting your perspective and seeing your wound with compassion rather than criticism. After years of practice and therapy, I've gotten so much better at this. I can look back on moments, like the time I said something awkward or overthought a conversation, and laugh at myself—not in mockery but in a way that disarms the power of guilt and shame.

Take, for example, the conversation I had with the podcaster. I remember feeling nervous, and in that nervousness, my mouth started moving faster than my brain. For a while, I judged myself harshly for it, thinking I'd messed up or sounded foolish. But now, with a little distance and self-awareness, I can giggle at that moment. I wasn't being mean or malicious—I was just a little scared, and that's okay! It's okay to be scared. It's okay to have moments where your humanity shines through in all its beautiful, messy imperfection. In fact, I've come to love that about myself. When I'm scared, I tend to speak quickly—it's part of who I am, and it's a reminder that I'm alive, feeling, and growing.

When we laugh at our wounds and give them some love, we take away their power to control us. Humor creates space for grace, and grace allows us to see ourselves as God sees us—not as broken or unworthy but as beloved. It's in this practice of kindness toward ourselves that we begin to transform judgment into acceptance, guilt into learning, and shame into growth. And that, my friend, is worth laughing about.

The challenge for all of us is to resist the temptation to shove our wound into the box of judgment and shame. That box is heavy, suffocating, and unhelpful, filled with lies that tell us our wound is something to hide or fix out of fear. Instead, the real work is to place our wound in the box of love and acceptance. The love and acceptance box is profoundly different. It says, "I love you and accept you, even when I don't fully understand you." This simple yet powerful affirmation creates space for grace, and grace is one of the most transformative tools we have on the journey toward wisdom and healing.

When we place our wound in the love and acceptance box, something remarkable begins to happen. Grace gives us the freedom to stop fighting our wound and start getting to know it. It allows us to approach our wound with curiosity instead of condemnation. From this perspective, we can see the edges of the wound more clearly, gaining insight into how it got there in the first place. Grace also helps us separate what is real about our wound from what is exaggerated or distorted by fear, insecurity, or false narratives. Without the fog of judgment and shame, we can discern the truth about our experiences with clarity.

The power of this shift isn't limited to how we view our own wounds—it extends to how we see others. When we practice love and acceptance toward ourselves, we naturally begin to offer that same grace to those around us. Instead of viewing their wounds or flaws through a lens of judgment, we see them with empathy and understanding. This perspective fosters deeper relationships and allows for greater connection, both with ourselves and with others.

Guilt and shame, on the other hand, distort everything. They act like smudged or cracked lenses, making it impossible to see clearly. When we allow ourselves to be covered in guilt and shame, we lose sight of the truth. These feelings weigh us down and keep us stuck, unable to move forward. But when we set down guilt and shame and embrace love and acceptance, we're no longer bound by the narratives that have held us captive. We free ourselves to explore, understand, and even celebrate the parts of us that we once tried to hide.

On the other side of this acceptance lies something extraordinary—our greatest gift. When we look at our wound with love and grace, we start to see how it has shaped not just our pain but also our potential. The wound is no longer a mark of brokenness but a source of strength, insight, and compassion. It's the place where our story begins to intersect with our purpose. That's when the real transformation begins.

On the other side of your wound is your greatest gift.

The redemptive nature of Christ becomes clear when we grasp the profound impact of sin, allowing us to fully embrace His transformative power. From Genesis to Revelation, Scripture paints a consistent picture: What the Enemy intends for evil, God redeems for good. This truth doesn't just apply to the grand narrative of humanity—it also applies to the personal wounds we carry. On the other side of what feels broken, painful, and deeply personal is something God has transformed into a vital part of who you are. That very wound, once a source of hurt, becomes the foundation of your greatest gift.

In my experience, this makes sense. As humans, we naturally compensate for areas in our lives where we've experienced pain or hurt. For example, if someone grows up feeling neglected, they may develop a gift for making others feel seen and valued because they know firsthand the pain of feeling invisible. This overcompensation isn't simply reactionary; it's redemptive. It's a way of ensuring that the pain we've experienced doesn't perpetuate itself in the lives of others. We see this phenomenon often in generational patterns, particularly in parenting. A generation that endured harsh discipline may embrace gentle parenting as a way to ensure their children experience something different. While this isn't a commentary on specific parenting styles, it illustrates a broader truth: Our experiences of pain often inspire us to create something better, more loving, and more redemptive.

Theologically, this theme runs throughout Scripture as a central narrative of God's story. Consider Peter, who denied Christ three times in his darkest moment of fear and failure. In John's Gospel, we see Jesus lovingly reinstate Peter, asking him three times to affirm his love and commissioning him to shepherd His people (John 21). What was once a moment of betrayal was transformed into a cornerstone of Peter's ministry as the rock upon which the church was built. Redemption isn't just something God does; it's who He is. Just as Peter's failure was redeemed for God's glory so too is your wound. Through the blood of the Lamb that was slain, your wound has been redeemed, and in that redemption, God has given you an incredible gift.

All of this leads us to one of the most important and undeniable truths:

On the other side of your wound is your greatest gift.

This phenomenon occurs because the subconscious mind naturally seeks to protect itself from repeating the pain of the wound. When we experience hurt, our brain responds by striving to avoid anything that might recreate or perpetuate that pain. This protective mechanism often leads to overcompensation, where we develop strengths and behaviors that counteract the source of our wound. For instance, if someone grew up feeling unheard or dismissed, they may develop a remarkable gift for listening and making others feel valued. It's the brain's way of ensuring that the pain once endured doesn't inflict itself upon others or resurface in their own life. In this sense, our gifting becomes an adaptive response, a subconscious effort to transform pain into purpose.

Theologically, this aligns beautifully with the character of God as the redeemer and healer. Scripture consistently shows us a God who doesn't waste pain but instead uses it as a pathway to transformation and growth. God's redemptive work takes what the Enemy meant for harm and turns it into something good—not just for us but for others. Through His healing power, the wounds we carry are not only mended but also transformed into tools for His glory. Our greatest gifts are often born out of this redemptive process, as God reshapes what was once broken into something beautiful and life-giving.

Whether you lean more toward the clinical explanation or the theological one, the truth remains that your greatest gift is often found on the other side of your wound. The connection between the two is profound, and understanding this relationship is key to uncovering the identity of your wound. When you begin to explore your gifting—what comes naturally to you and what brings joy and purpose to your life—you can often trace its roots back to the very pain that shaped you. This process of discovery is both humbling and empowering, as it reveals not only the depth of your wound but also the incredible potential God has placed within you to bring light and hope to the world.

When discussing the idea of wounding, people often have a hard time identifying what the wound is or how it shows up in their life. In the course of that discussion, I always ask them for their greatest gift, "What is your best gift to the world?" While on some occasions that stumps someone, most people (with a little encouragement) can identify their greatest gift with greater ease than their wound. Now, to be clear, when I talk about the greatest gift, I'm not talking about physical attributes. If I was standing in front of Joe Burrow (Who Dey!) and I asked him what his greatest gift is, I wouldn't accept the answer to throw a football. That's a physical gift. The gift I am talking about is the one thing that you are truly gifted at, your superpower. The superpower you have to give to the world. It's an emotional superpower, something that resonates from the depths of your being. It is the "thing" you do for other people that when they think of you, they remember. It's the gift you have to give back to the world. The emotional gift. What you do for other people.

Do you remember my wound? I want to be seen. I want people to appreciate me, and I have moments where I am terrified that I don't matter to the world. So, if the statement *On the other side of your wound is your greatest gift* is true, then my gift is going to be related to my wound. In my case, it's easy—my greatest gift to the world is that I have a unique ability to see people at their core. I often do marriage coaching, and within the first ten minutes, I can identify the tension points in their marriage. It can be a little freaky; sometimes, couples say, "Have you been following me around?!" And the answer is, no, but I have a gift. I can see people. I didn't do anything to deserve this gift; it is simply the way Christ has redeemed my wound. And to be blunt, you have a gift too. Christ did not skip over you when He was redeeming wounds. Everyone has a gift. Even if you can't figure out your wound (yet).

One of the benefits of doing this work for years before writing this book is that I've had the chance to observe and recognize patterns not just in my own life but in the lives of others. One of the most profound realizations I've had is this: The Enemy, whether you call him Satan, sin, or something else, is not a creator. He doesn't innovate; he corrupts. His tactics are recycled, predictable, and designed to exploit our vulnerabilities. Over time, you begin to notice the wounds people carry often stem from similar sources: rejection, fear, inadequacy, shame, or abandonment. The Enemy uses these wounds as tools to divide, discourage, and distort. But there's hope because, while the Enemy cannot create, our Father in Heaven is the ultimate Creator.

Christ doesn't just leave us in our brokenness; He steps into it with creativity and power, redeeming our wounds in ways we could never imagine. His work is never formulaic or one size fits all. Instead, He meets each of us uniquely, crafting a redemptive story that transforms pain into purpose. What was once a source of shame becomes a source of strength; what was once a place of brokenness becomes a platform for connection and healing. This creative redemption is not just evidence of God's power but also a testament to His deep love for us. He doesn't just patch us up—He makes us new.

When you start to see the patterns in others' wounds, it's like being given a new set of eyes. You begin to look past surface behaviors and defenses to see people at a heart level. You recognize that their reactions, struggles, and even their gifts often trace back to the same kind of pain you've wrestled with in your own life. This understanding doesn't just make you more compassionate—it changes the way you operate in relationships. Instead of being reactive, you become intentional. Instead of judging, you approach others with grace. You stop seeing their wounds as liabilities and start seeing them as opportunities for connection and growth.

What's even more transformative is how this perspective shifts your own heart. As you grow in your ability to see patterns in others, you'll find yourself more attuned to God's redemptive work in your life. The same Creator who redeems their wounds is at work in you, too, and when you begin to understand that, it doesn't just change how you see others—it changes how you see yourself. It reminds you that you are not defined by your wounds but by the Creator who is faithfully redeeming them. This work is life-giving, not just for you but for every relationship you enter. It equips you to be a vessel of Christ's creative redemption, bringing healing and hope to those around you. Here are some examples.

Imagine you were the oldest child, and you grew up in a home where you felt a lot of pressure. That pressure sometimes means you have a tendency to believe that in order to receive, love you have to perform. Your wound is that "performance = love," and you can be afraid that if you don't show up for people in a certain kind of way, you aren't loveable. Well, let's talk about the gift in order to connect to that wound. The gift is usually that you love people in a huge way; your love is unconditional, and while you believe you must act a certain way to receive love, you'll happily give away love. So, if you have a "performance = love" wound, then I would bet you have a great way of loving people unconditionally.

Another example would be someone who grew up in what felt like chaos. Maybe there was a lot of moving, or maybe you felt like everyone was on pins and needles in your home. Again, remember, your wound isn't about malicious intent, just a broken interpretation of what happened while you were being formed in the world. So, if you grew up in a home that felt like it was full of chaos, then it is possible (or probable) that your gift to the world is order. You have a unique ability to order things in such a way that everyone feels safe and secure. You probably feel most comfortable in control and want to have a plan for how the situation or day is going to go. Your gift is order, and it is built out of living in chaos.

One more example, let's say one of your parents worked a lot during your childhood. Again, not malicious intent, just the reality that as a kid, it felt like one of your parents was gone all the time. If you grew up in a home where that was your interpretation, then your wound might be that you felt left or abandoned as a child. So, as a result, a redemption of that wound could be loyalty. You might be one of those "ride or die" friends. Through it all, you never leave your people, and you are there for them no matter what the circumstance. This is the redemption of your gift, and it is beautiful. Your gift is loyalty, and it is built out of feeling left.

The process of defining gifts and wounds is ultimately about building self-awareness. This journey is not about fitting into a mold or adhering to a rigid formula—it's about discovering your unique story. The examples provided are just common patterns, not the definitive guide for every person. Your experience may look different, and that's okay. Life is complex, and sometimes wounds overlap or blend, creating a more nuanced picture. When you factor in big "T" traumas—significant, life-altering events— the process can shift entirely, layering new dimensions of pain and resilience into the equation.

To begin identifying your gift, take time to reflect, but also invite the perspectives of those closest to you. Ask your spouse, your closest friends, or your trusted colleagues. Often, they see strengths and gifts in you that you can't recognize in yourself because your self-perception is clouded by your wound and your own self-doubt. The person staring back at you in the mirror may offer a skewed perspective, shaped by years of internal criticism or fear. In other words, don't rely solely on the advice of the person in the mirror. Self-awareness grows when we bring others into the process, allowing them to reflect back the truths we may struggle to see.

As you start to identify and understand the other side of your wound—your gift—you open the door to loving yourself more wholly. The wound itself doesn't get to define you any more than your gift does, but when you start to see the interconnectedness of the two, you gain a fuller picture of who you are. Your wound and your gift are not opposing forces; they are part of the same story, working together to shape your identity. The wisest leaders in the world aren't those without wounds—they are those who have cultivated intimacy with their wounds. They know what triggers emotional spikes, what vulnerabilities exist, and how their gifts emerge from the same place of pain.

This intimacy with your wound allows you to move beyond mere understanding to acceptance. You begin to see your wound not as a limitation but as a part of what makes you uniquely equipped to lead, love, and serve. You can even love your wound because you recognize the gift that has grown through it. When you embrace your wound fully—its edges, its history, its role in shaping your gifts—you can also begin to surrender the feelings surrounding it. The guilt, shame, and fear that once clung to your wound lose their power. In their place, you find grace, compassion, and a deeper sense of self. This is where healing begins and where your wound becomes not just a part of your story but a source of strength and purpose.

Over the years, the more I've come to accept my wound, the less shame and guilt I carry about my entire existence. Accepting my wound hasn't made it disappear nor has it minimized its impact—but it has changed the way I see myself. I've come to embrace the truth that I am both broken and gifted, and these two realities are not at odds. They coexist, shaping who I am and how I navigate the world. My brokenness doesn't disqualify me, and my gifting doesn't make me invincible. Together, they form a more honest, authentic picture of who I am—a person in progress, striving daily to be more like Christ.

What I've learned is that Jesus loves me fully, exactly as I am, but He also loves me so much that He refuses to leave me there. His love is not passive or permissive; it is active and transformative. It's a love that meets me in my brokenness and walks with me toward healing and growth. This journey of becoming more like Christ isn't a quick fix or a one-time event—it's a process, a lifelong invitation to grow in grace and intimacy with Him. And in that process, my prayer is that my wound becomes something I know deeply and accept fully, not as a source of shame but as a part of my story.

At the same time, I pray that my gift becomes more transparent, not hidden behind fear or pride but offered freely to the world as an extension of God's redemptive work in my life. To be a leader who understands and accepts both the wound and the gift is no small task. It requires humility, courage, and a willingness to embrace the tension of being both broken and redeemed. But I believe that this is the kind of leadership Christ calls us to—leadership that is honest about its weaknesses, rooted in grace, and open to the transformative power of God's love. This is the leadership I strive for, knowing that in my weakness, His strength is made perfect and in my wounds, His glory is revealed.

Exercise:

1. **Journaling Prompt:** Write a letter of acceptance to your wound, acknowledging its presence and the gifts it has shaped in you.

2. **Emotional Awareness:** Begin to think about the wound in the people closest to you: How can you get to know them on a deeper level?

3. **Challenge:** Ask three close friends or family members to share what they see as your greatest gifts. Reflect on how these gifts might relate to your wounds.

Leading with Your Wound

*For we do not have a high priest who is unable to empathize
with our weaknesses, but we have one who has been tempted
in every way, just as we are—yet he did not sin.*

*Let us then approach God's throne of grace with confidence,
so that we may receive mercy and find grace to help us in our
time of need.*

– Hebrews 4:15–16

One of my favorite stories in all of Scripture comes from John 13, a passage that has shaped not only my faith but also my work—so much so that I named my business and podcast in its honor: *Follow2Lead.* In John 13, we see Jesus sitting with His disciples during what would become one of His final moments with them. Then, in an act that is as profound as it is unexpected, Jesus does something extraordinary. The text says, *"Jesus knew that he had come from God and was returning to God; so..." (John 13:3-4).* That small word "so" is underlined and circled in my Bible. It's a simple conjunction, but its significance is massive. It ties together two critical truths: Jesus knew His identity, and because He knew who He was, He was able to take action in a way that defied cultural expectations and demonstrated servant leadership.

What Jesus does next is nothing short of revolutionary. He stands up, takes a basin of water, and begins to wash the feet of His disciples. In first-century culture, washing feet was the task of the lowest servant, an act reserved for those with no social status or authority. Yet here is Jesus—the Son of God, the Savior of the world—kneeling before His followers, taking on the posture of a servant. Why? Because He knew who He was in the Father. The text is clear: Jesus was secure in His identity. He knew He had come from God and would return to God. This deep clarity about His identity informed His actions, even in the most humbling of circumstances.

This story holds a profound truth about leadership: Identity informs action. Jesus didn't wash the disciples' feet to prove something about Himself or to earn their respect. He did it because He already knew who He was. His leadership wasn't driven by insecurity or a need for validation—it flowed from the deep well of His relationship with the Father. Even as He faced the shadow of the cross, Jesus was unwavering in His purpose because He was unwavering in His identity.

That's what I want for you, too. I want you to have the clarity of identity that empowers you to lead with humility, confidence, and purpose. When you know who you are—when your identity is grounded in something unshakable—it frees you to take action that aligns with your values and calling. You don't have to chase approval or prove your worth because you already know where you stand. Like Jesus, your identity becomes the foundation for everything you do, enabling you to serve others, face challenges, and lead with integrity. That's the kind of leadership that transforms not only your own life but the lives of those around you.

Far too often, we find ourselves operating out of a position of confusion rather than clarity. We move through life reacting to circumstances instead of responding with purpose simply because we haven't taken the time to know who we are. Our identity feels elusive, buried under layers of roles we play, expectations we try to meet, and wounds we've never fully explored. Without a clear understanding of who we are, how can we possibly lead others well? Leadership begins with identity, and when we lack clarity in our own, we risk leading from a place of insecurity, fear, or confusion.

This truth applies to everyone regardless of your title or role. Whether you're a Fortune 500 CEO handling her business with a fierce tenacity or a stay-at-home dad managing the day-to-day chaos of family life, you are leading someone. Leadership isn't about position or power—it's about influence. If people are looking to you for guidance, wisdom, or direction, then you are a leader. And as a leader, the time you invest in understanding your identity is not just an investment in yourself; it's an investment in those you lead.

When you take the time to be clear about who you are—your values, your strengths, your wounds, and your gifts—you lead with greater intention and authenticity. Clarity of identity gives you a solid foundation to make decisions, set priorities, and navigate challenges. It helps you lead from a place of confidence rather than self-doubt, and it allows you to connect with those you lead on a deeper level. People are drawn to leaders who know themselves because they bring stability, purpose, and integrity to every interaction.

On the flip side, when we fail to do the work of knowing ourselves, we often lead out of confusion, letting our unresolved wounds or insecurities dictate our actions. This can create an environment of inconsistency or mistrust, making it harder for those we lead to thrive. But when we lead from a place of clarity, we inspire others to find clarity in their own lives. Our leadership becomes a reflection of the work we've done to understand and embrace who we are, and that kind of leadership is transformative—for ourselves and for those we have the privilege to influence.

One of the greatest leaders I ever had the pleasure of serving with was Chaplain Charles Causey.[1] Chaplain Causey has this unique ability to bring people along, and in that process, he makes you feel valued and heard. I don't think he has any special superpowers, but I do think he has spent time in reflection and awareness to know who he is. When I first met him, we were stationed in Ft. Snelling, Minnesota. It wasn't what I would call a luxurious location, and while we both knew I would only be there for a year, one of the things he did right away was bring me into his family to the point that his kids often felt like my younger siblings, and I would hang out there regularly. Because he and Lauri (his wonderful wife) were clear about who they were in Christ, they could open their home and let me see how they live with no filters attached. They were so clear about their identity that Charles and Lauri even offered to read the Bible with me and Karen for a year. Every day, I would come into the office, and Charles would sit me down on his couch to talk about the reading from the night before. To be clear, this wasn't one of the objectives of the job; this wasn't part of the plan. This was a leader who was

---

1. For more about Chaplain Charles Causey, go to www.causeybooks.com.

clear about who he was and could see a young man (me) who was still sorting through his beliefs/values/identity. Charles could do these things because he was clear about who he was. Lauri could use her amazing gift of hospitality because she was clear about who she was in Christ.

The most effective leaders aren't defined by a particular set of talents or skills. While those abilities are important, what truly sets them apart is their deep understanding of who they are and what they bring to the table. Leadership isn't about perfection; it's about authenticity and self-awareness. Leaders who are clear about their identity, strengths, and limitations have a grounded confidence that allows them to lead with purpose and integrity. Conversely, leaders who lack self-awareness often struggle to connect with others, make consistent decisions, or navigate challenges effectively.

Your own self-awareness will either be the ceiling or the floor of your ability to lead others. If your self-awareness is shallow, it becomes a ceiling—a limiting factor that holds you back. But if your self-awareness is deep and intentional, it becomes the floor—a strong foundation that elevates your leadership to new heights. The fact that you're already reading a book about wounding suggests that you're willing to do the work of looking at who you are. That willingness is a powerful first step, but I want to challenge you to take it further.

Don't just stop at self-reflection; dive deeper into the process of understanding how you show up as a leader. Take the time to evaluate how your strengths, weaknesses, wounds, and gifts influence your interactions with others. And here's where it gets even more impactful: Ask the people you lead for feedback. Ask them, "What's it like to be on the other side of me?" This question requires vulnerability and courage, but it's one of the most transformative things you can do as a leader.

When you ask this question with an open heart, you gain invaluable insight into how your leadership is perceived. You may discover strengths you didn't fully recognize, or you may uncover blind spots that need attention. Either way, this feedback helps you align your leadership with the values and vision you want to embody. It also demonstrates to those you lead that you value their experience and are committed to growing for their benefit, not just your own. That kind of humility and intentionality creates trust, respect, and a deeper connection, which are the hallmarks of truly effective leadership.

As a lead pastor, my wound would show up in some pretty crazy ways. Since my wound is all about feeling seen (it makes sense I'd pick a job that gives me a microphone), every decision I make as a leader could bump up against that wound. Am I the face of the organization? Am I the right person to deliver the message? Is this about me, or is this about the mission? Those are real questions, and they are important questions, but here is the kicker: When the questions are about me, I may not be the best person to answer them. This is where having a great team comes into play and not just a great team, but a team that is honest and vulnerable about what gifts/skills you have as a leader. Find people in your organization that love the mission enough to call you out on the moments when you are leading out of your wound. And when you find those people, remember that this idea of "calling you out" is a tension to be managed. Some days, the "calling out" will make great sense; other days, it will feel like someone hit you in the head with a two-by-four. Leading out of your wound isn't an equation that is simple and clear; rather, it is a messy tension.

Some days, you'll nail the self-awareness; some days, you'll never see the wound coming at you. Both days will exist over the course of your life. This is why who you surround yourself with matters deeply. Their view of your wound is imperative for clarity. However, not all friends are created equal (and that's okay).

In my experience, there are three stereotypical types of friends. All the types are important, but as a leader, you would benefit from knowing who is who. Internet friends, role friends, and real friends are how I think about them in my life, and of course, there are always exceptions to the rules, but for the most part, everyone fits into one of these three categories. These categories are your own classifications; feel free to use whatever labels make the most sense for you. In my mind, there are three circles: the outer, the middle, and the inner.

Internet friends: This group of friends is most often distant from your heart. I'm not suggesting that you can't form deep bonds or connections or even develop amazing, deep relationships with people on the internet. What I am referring to is the large part of the internet that you don't engage with other than to wish them a happy birthday or to like the picture of their kid they posted. They are super important to your network, and they are the ones who are best categorized because you only keep up with them through the internet. Do yourself a favor and don't put any judgement around this; you need internet friends. LinkedIn, Facebook, or Insta—internet friends will help support your dreams and criticize you the loudest. When it comes to the access of your wound, internet friends have a distinct way of bumping up against it. They are the ones who often have thoughts about what you are doing even though they don't even know who you are at your core. Just remember this: You don't have any responsibility to do anything for internet friends. It's not the kind of relationship that commands attention unless you want to give it attention. Be careful not to let internet friends speak too much into your life or eventually you'll feel a little bit like a ping pong ball.

Role friends: Role friends are a part of your life because you play a very specific role in their life. This is most often the people you work with or the people you see on a regular basis, but you didn't intentionally choose them. Extended family can sometimes fit into this description. It's good to appreciate and support the role they play in your life but hold it with the right amount of tension. Role friends get to speak into your life about some things but not everything. For example, having a good group of role friends is essential for leadership at the workplace, but they may not share the same values as you, so they may not get to comment on how you make a decision at home or with your kids. One thing I can guarantee—role friends will bump up against your wound. Some of them may even be able to help you see/understand how that plays out in your life. Role friends are an incredible gift, and I know for sure that I wouldn't be who I am today without them. When you form a team, I recommend looking for people who have different wounds than you, and I know that can be difficult to see, but the more you spend time with your wound, the easier it will be to see the wounds of others. Having a dynamic and diverse team of role friends is one of the most rewarding things I have ever done as a leader.

Real friends: Real friends are exactly what they sound like, "ride or die." They are the people in your life that can speak right to your wound, and because they have been there through multiple seasons, they have earned the ability to see you and be heard by you. In my life, I have a couple of groups of people who are my real friends. They know my crazy. I can be unfiltered with them. And through it all, they love me and understand my wound. They are the guys who I don't have to be a certain person with; they get the unfiltered version of me. Annie F. Downs (podcaster and author) says it like this, "Everyone should have a private life, no one should have a secret life." Annie's words resonate with me at a deep level, and my real friends are the ones who know everything.

ALL of these friends are important. They are the ones who will help you see your wound with greater clarity and will give you the opportunity to reflect on what's going on inside you. From the Christian perspective, the most dangerous leader is the one who thinks they can do it on their own. In Luke's Gospel, Jesus sends out the 72 in pairs, and since they could have certainly covered more ground individually, it stands to reason that going together allowed them to go further. Being with people changes who we are and sustains us when life is beating down the door. Understanding your wound is the first step; sharing it with the real friends in your life is the next steps, and eventually, sharing with role friends. The more intimate you get with your wound, the more you'll be able to share the emotional truth in a healthy and productive way.

Sharing the emotional truth is one of the most important skills a leader can develop. While the physical truth—the factual recounting of events—is essential in some contexts, like drafting a police report or conducting a detailed analysis, it often falls short in addressing the heart of an issue. The emotional truth, on the other hand, delves deeper into the human experience. It shifts the focus from *what happened* to *how it felt,* providing a lens that is often more relevant and impactful for effective communication and leadership.

The physical truth might go something like this: *"This person walked in, said this, and then I responded by doing this."* It's a straightforward account of events, important for clarity and chronology but limited in scope. It doesn't tell us why the interaction mattered, how it impacted you, or what it revealed about the people involved. For most leaders, this level of detail doesn't create connection—it's a surface-level recounting that leaves the emotional undercurrent untouched.

The emotional truth, by contrast, is much richer. It goes beyond actions and words to share the feelings behind them. It might sound like this: *"When this person walked in and said that I immediately felt dismissed. I started to feel anxious, then defensive, and I responded in a way that didn't align with my values because I was overwhelmed by those emotions."* This explanation reveals not only what happened but why it mattered to you and how it shaped your response. It invites understanding and empathy, both of which are critical for building trust and connection.

Leaders who focus on sharing the emotional truth cultivate deeper relationships with their teams and those they influence. The emotional truth acknowledges vulnerability, something that fosters trust and shows authenticity. It allows others to see not just the actions but the humanity behind the actions. When leaders share their emotional truth, they model emotional intelligence, demonstrating that it's okay to name feelings and reflect on their impact.

The emotional truth also carries more weight than the physical truth because it touches the shared human experience. Facts alone may inform, but emotions resonate. When you share your emotional truth, you create space for others to share theirs, leading to more meaningful conversations and stronger connections.

As a leader, this skill helps you navigate conflict, inspire your team, and make decisions that are not just logical but also empathetic. By focusing on the emotional truth, you shift from merely recounting events to truly engaging with the people you lead.

Let me give you an example of the physical truth:

> *Recently, my oldest child came home from college for Thanksgiving. He landed on Tuesday and stayed till Sunday. It was great having him home. We talked, he relaxed, and I enjoyed watching him connect with the family in the way he had for the previous 18 years of his life. We took him to the airport on Sunday morning, and he returned to college to finish out the year.*

In that example, I gave you the physical truth of what happened. I explained it clearly, and you know what took place. Here is an example of the emotional truth:

> *Recently, my oldest child came home from college for Thanksgiving—I was so excited to see him! The stay was short, but what a joy it was to have his presence. My heart felt full watching him connect with the family. Nothing quite fills my tank like having all my kids underneath one roof. Dropping him off was sad, but I was also full of pride knowing what God has in store for him.*

The physical truth can describe the situation; the emotional truth describes the situation of your heart. Good leaders learn how to tell both.

As a leader, your responsibility doesn't stop at understanding your own wound—it extends to recognizing and responding to the wounds of the people on your team. Leadership isn't just about achieving goals or hitting metrics; it's about building relationships that empower others to thrive. This requires you to look beyond tasks and productivity and truly see the individuals you lead. It means investing time in getting to know them, not just as employees or contributors but as people with unique stories, experiences, and challenges. This shift from a task-oriented mindset to a people-oriented one is what separates transactional leaders from transformational ones.

To truly understand the wounds of the people on your team, you have to become intentional about listening. This isn't just about hearing their words—it's about listening with empathy and curiosity. These two tools are invaluable for leaders who want to connect with their teams on a deeper level.

Empathy allows you to step into someone else's shoes and feel what they're feeling. It's about more than just sympathy or acknowledging that someone is struggling—it's about actively seeking to understand their perspective and emotional experience. When you approach your team with empathy, you create a safe environment where they feel seen, heard, and valued. This intentionality fosters trust, which is essential for any healthy team dynamic. Empathy also helps you recognize patterns in behavior that might be tied to deeper wounds. For example, a team member who consistently avoids conflict might have a wound tied to past experiences of rejection or criticism. Recognizing these patterns allows you to lead with compassion and intentionality, offering support that meets them where they are.

Curiosity complements empathy by encouraging you to ask questions and seek deeper understanding. While empathy helps you connect emotionally, curiosity helps you explore the "why" behind someone's actions or feelings. It invites you to ask open-ended questions like, *What's going on for you right now?* or *Can you help me understand how this situation is affecting you?* These kinds of questions show your team members that you care about more than just their output—you care about them as individuals. Curiosity also helps you avoid making assumptions about their wounds or motivations. Instead of jumping to conclusions, you take the time to learn their unique stories and perspectives.

Together, empathy and curiosity enable you to see the wounds of your team members without judgment or bias. They allow you to lead with a relational focus that acknowledges the humanity of your team while still driving results. When you take the time to understand the wounds of those you lead, you can help them harness their own gifts and strengths, creating a team dynamic built on trust, growth, and shared purpose. This kind of leadership doesn't just create better outcomes—it creates better people.

Judgment is one of those subtle but powerful barriers to growth. The more we judge, the more we solidify assumptions about how things *should* be or how people *should* act. This creates a rigid framework in our minds that leaves little room for exploration, understanding, or flexibility. Judgment becomes a mental shortcut, a way to quickly categorize actions, decisions, or even people as "right" or "wrong," "good" or "bad," "stupid" or "smart." While this might feel efficient in the moment, it ultimately limits our ability to see the full picture and connect meaningfully with others.

When it comes to leadership, judgment is particularly damaging because it becomes a significant barrier to curiosity and empathy. You cannot approach someone with genuine curiosity or engage with them empathetically if you've already made up your mind about their actions or motivations. Judgment closes doors that curiosity and empathy are meant to open. If you've decided that a team member's decision was "stupid," for example, you're unlikely to ask questions like, *What led you to that choice?* or *How did you approach this problem?* Instead, you've already dismissed their actions without understanding their perspective or intent.

For me, this challenge is very real. I often find myself having knee-jerk reactions to evaluate situations through the binary lens of "stupid" or "smart." It's a voice in my head that seems to speak before I have a chance to catch it: *That was stupid.* or *that was genius.* I wish I could say that voice didn't exist, but it does, and it's a constant reminder of the work I still need to do. Judgment can feel automatic, almost instinctual, but as a leader striving to be more Christ-like, I know it's something I have to fight against every single day.

Being a Christ-like leader means resisting the urge to categorize and instead choosing to connect. Jesus, throughout His ministry, demonstrated an extraordinary ability to engage with people based not on assumptions or societal judgments but on love, grace, and understanding. He saw beyond surface actions to the heart of each person, offering compassion where others offered condemnation. This is the model I strive to follow, even when it's hard. It means pausing before reacting, questioning my assumptions, and choosing curiosity over critique.

Judgment, left unchecked, isolates us from the people we're meant to lead and serve, but when we resist judgment and embrace curiosity and empathy, we create space for growth—not just for others but for ourselves as well. It's in this space that we can become better leaders, better teammates, and better reflections of Christ's love. Every day, I work to quiet that judgmental voice and replace it with one that seeks to understand. It's not always easy, but it's always worth it.

Building the muscle of empathy and curiosity starts with one simple rule: Ask more questions than you make statements. Podcasting has been an incredible tool in developing that muscle in my life. Through over 375 podcast episodes, I've learned how to ask penetrating questions and let me be clear—you can too. You don't even need to start a podcast to do it. You just need to follow these simple ideas:

1. **Chase curiosity.** Whatever sticks out to you, pull the metaphorical string. Chase curiosity and see where it takes you. Follow it to the natural conclusion, and always be willing to surrender the destination. When I don't care about where I am going, I always enjoy the process of getting there a bit more.

2. **Ask questions about the emotional truth, not the physical truth**. If you want to get to know the people that are on your team, don't just ask them about what they did this weekend; ask them how they felt about the weekend. I promise, it's a different answer than you would ever expect, and through that process, you'll get to hear the heart of your team in a different way. Physical truth questions are great if you are building a report on an event; emotional truth questions build a rapport with a person's heart. Some great emotional truth questions are: How did that feel? What did that experience teach you? Where do you see yourself in the current situation?

3. **Listen with your whole heart**. One of the most embarrassing moments of my life was when this sweet, old church lady came to me in the church lobby and said, "Pastor Tony, I don't ever feel like you are listening when I am talking to you. It feels like you are already moving on to the next conversation." She was right; I was think-

ing about the next conversation. Since that sobering day, I've met dozens of leaders who suffer from the same disease. We cannot be empathetic or curious if we aren't actively listening. Take the time to be present with the people you lead, and I promise you'll begin to see part of them that you never knew even existed.

If we truly model our lives after Christ and look to Him as the ultimate leader, one of the most remarkable things we notice is His mastery of asking questions. Throughout the Gospels, Jesus frequently asked thought-provoking, open-ended questions that challenged people to think deeply, reflect on their hearts, and arrive at their own conclusions. He didn't rush to provide answers or lecture those around Him; instead, He used questions to guide, teach, and transform. Questions like, *"Who do you say I am?"* (Matthew 16:15), *"What do you want me to do for you?"* (Mark 10:51), and *"Why are you so afraid?"* (Matthew 8:26) weren't just rhetorical—they were invitations to self-discovery and deeper faith.

What's striking is that Jesus often asked questions without directly answering them. This wasn't because He lacked the knowledge but because He knew the power of questions to spark growth. By asking instead of telling, Jesus gave people the opportunity to wrestle with their own thoughts, beliefs, and motivations. This approach not only deepened their understanding but also empowered them to take ownership of their faith and decisions.

The beauty of being a good question asker, as Jesus modeled, is that it reflects wisdom without arrogance. The wisest people I know rarely give definitive answers. Instead, they consistently ask great questions that lead others to discover truth for themselves. There's a humility in this approach—it acknowledges that people often learn best when they are invited into the process rather than being handed a solution. Asking questions also communicates trust and respect. It says, *I value your thoughts and believe you're capable of finding the answer.*

For leaders, this is an invaluable lesson. Too often, we feel pressure to have all the answers, thinking that's what makes us effective. But in reality, leadership isn't about being the smartest person in the room; it's about empowering others to grow. Asking thoughtful, intentional questions is one of the most effective ways to do that. Questions invite collaboration, spark creativity, and encourage deeper engagement. They help people see their own potential and navigate challenges with greater clarity.

When we follow Christ's example and prioritize asking over answering, we lead with both wisdom and humility. We create an environment where people feel heard, valued, and equipped to take ownership of their growth. Perhaps most importantly, we reflect the heart of Christ—a leader who didn't just provide solutions but transformed lives by inviting people to think, reflect, and discover truth for themselves. In a world that often prioritizes quick answers, choosing to ask great questions is a countercultural act of leadership that can make a profound and lasting impact.

Exercise:

1. **Journaling Prompt:**

   - Think of a recent decision or interaction you had as a leader. Ask yourself:

     - Did my wound influence my response or decision?

     - How did my wound affect the people on my team?

     - Was I even aware of my wound in the moment, or did it catch me by surprise after the fact?

     - How might my gift have shaped a more balanced approach?

   - In retrospect, write down any observations on your leadership style. Moving forward, how can you use more of your gift and still honor your wound?

2. **Emotional Awareness:**

   - Ask three people who work closely with you, "What's it like to be on the other side of me?"

   - Use their feedback to identify areas where your wound may unintentionally affect your leadership and areas where your gift shines.

3. **Challenge:**

   - Identify a project or task where you struggled as a leader.

   - Reflect on whether your wound or gift was influencing the challenge.

   - Create a plan for how you can better align your leadership with your gift in future tasks.

The Wisest People
I Know

*The heart of the discerning acquires knowledge, for the ears
of the wise seek it out.*

– Proverbs 18:15

My daughter is my princess. When she was born, I pulled her brothers aside and said, "Whatever you do, protect your sister." They, of course, nodded and agreed. When Shiloh got to be about eight, I pulled the boys aside again and said, "Protect yourself, I have nothing for ya!" And while I joke about that idea often, what happened is that Shiloh became a warrior princess. She is strong, funny, and, like everyone in our family, carries strong opinions. During one particular season of her life, I was on a mission to try and get her to like hiking. The rest of the family enjoyed it, and Shiloh despised the idea of it. She didn't understand the thought that maybe we would just walk in the woods for enjoyment. In an effort to combat that idea, I created something called "Hiking Club." Hiking Club was two days a week, it was something we would do together, and it was laced with incentives that encouraged getting out and walking. One particular Hiking Club morning, she hadn't slept well the night before, and things were rather tragic from her perspective. She needed to use the bathroom, the port-o-potty wasn't clean enough, she wanted a snack, and the last thing she wanted to do was walk in the summer humidity. There were so many tears, so much frustration, so much suffering (from her perspective). In an effort to make it happen, I almost dragged her out to the middle of the hiking path and tried to trudge forward, only to eventually lose my ever-loving mind and become furious with my princess, which only ended in both of us getting back in the truck grumpy and disappointed in each other.

To recap, I was angry that my ten-year-old daughter didn't want to do something, which she had routinely expressed to me. I was angry at her response that, which in hindsight, I knew was going to happen—she had already told me she didn't want to go! The moral of this story is not that we shouldn't have done Hiking Club; I think it's important to teach your kids to do hard things. The moral of the story is that my reaction was foolish. I knew what I was getting into, so when Shiloh bumped up against my wound, it is astonishing that I would get upset by it. I basically created the entire situation she didn't want to be in, and then I was mad that she didn't want to be there.

As leaders, many of us unknowingly set ourselves up for frustration by creating environments where we expect others to meet unspoken or unrealistic expectations—expectations they had no part in shaping. We design a workplace, a team dynamic, or even a culture based on what we value, how we think, and what motivates us. Then, we get upset when others don't respond to that environment the way we think they should. It's like setting the table for a meal no one asked for and then getting frustrated when they don't enjoy it.

One common frustration many leaders face is the emotional investment they have in their business or mission. We want people to treat it the way we do with the same passion, commitment, and sense of ownership. When they don't, it feels personal. We take it as a lack of respect or loyalty, and we pour energy into finding someone who will care as much as we do. This quest often leads to even more frustration, as we come to the harsh realization that no one will ever care about our business, our vision, or our goals in exactly the same way we do—because it's *our* business not theirs.

The problem is compounded by the fact that we sometimes have emotional reactions to the very situations we created. We expect people to thrive in an environment they didn't help shape, and we grow resentful when they don't. What we fail to see is that environments are not just about physical spaces or policies—they're about shared values, input, and emotional resonance. When people don't feel a sense of ownership or connection, it's unreasonable to expect them to bring the same level of care and commitment that we do.

I'm continually learning that this mindset is not just unrealistic—it's counterproductive. It's foolish to think we can unilaterally create an environment and then control someone else's emotional response to it. Leaders get to set the values and steer the culture. Then, the people in our community/work get to decide if they want to buy into it. People are not programmable robots; they are individuals with their own values, motivations, and emotional frameworks. Leadership is not about controlling how people feel or react—it's about inviting them into a process where they feel seen, heard, and valued. It's about co-creating an environment where they can bring their best selves to the table, not just conform to a space that was pre-designed without their input. Yes, as a leader, you will set the tone, but in the healthiest places I know, the tone is not a dictatorship—it's a conversation.

Instead, the wisest people I know are perfectly okay with you having whatever emotional response you want, while not letting it dictate their emotional response. Said another way, the wisest people in the world are not without wounds but rather possess such an intimacy with their wound that it doesn't get to make decisions in their life.

Even the greatest leaders in the world are wounded. They have "stuff." They have feelings, and they have to work through them just like the rest of us. What differentiates these leaders is that they are so intimate with their wound that they don't get scared when someone or something bumps up against it. Take the earlier story about Shiloh and Hiking Club—if I could go back in time, I would have just sat with my daughter and listened to her heart. I would have asked questions, and maybe I would have learned something that would have built empathy or leaned into curiosity. If I could have surrendered my emotional reaction, I could have been present with her to hear what her heart was really saying. Would that have made everything work? Would that have motivated her to hike that day? Probably not. But what it would have done is eliminated the possibility that I might damage our relationship with my emotional reaction. Fortunately, Shiloh and I have a great relationship, but the problem with an emotional reaction is that sometimes it can cause damage that can't be undone.

Wise people have emotions—deep, complex, and powerful emotions. No one on Earth is a robot, immune to the influence of feelings. But the difference between the wise and the foolish is not the presence or absence of emotions—it's how they navigate them. Wise individuals are intimately familiar with their emotions. They take the time to understand what they're feeling, process those emotions when and where it's safe, and respond intentionally rather than impulsively. They don't let others dictate how or when their emotions come out. Instead, they maintain control over their responses, ensuring their emotions serve their purpose rather than derail it.

Dr. Martin Luther King Jr. exemplified this balance of emotional depth and wisdom. By all accounts, he was a profoundly emotional man, moved by the injustices of his time and driven by a passionate desire for change. He ministered to people in their lowest moments, empathizing deeply with their pain and struggles. His speeches were filled with fiery conviction, reflecting the depth of his emotions and the weight of his mission. Yet, what set him apart was not just his passion but his ability to channel it with precision.

King's measured and thoughtful approach to adversity is what made him a transformational leader. He didn't suppress his emotions, nor did he let them spill out unchecked. Instead, he chose his words and actions carefully, ensuring that they aligned with his values and the goals of the civil rights movement. Even in the face of immense provocation—violence, injustice, and personal threats—he rarely allowed anger or frustration to dictate his response. His restraint wasn't a denial of his feelings but a mastery over them, allowing him to lead with strength and clarity.

This ability to balance emotion and wisdom gave King the credibility and authority to inspire millions. People saw in him not just a man who felt deeply but a leader who knew how to harness those feelings to create meaningful change. His emotional intelligence, combined with his strategic mind, allowed him to respond with love to hate, with peace to violence, and with justice to injustice. It's a lesson for all of us: Emotions are not a weakness—they are a strength when understood and stewarded well.

Wise leadership is not about avoiding emotions but about becoming so intimate with them that they serve as tools for connection, empathy, and vision. Like King, we are most impactful when we take the time to feel deeply, process thoughtfully, respond intentionally, and use our emotions to lead with purpose and integrity.

Wisdom is understanding that emotions are not meant to dictate our actions but to serve as decision points—moments that invite us to pause, reflect, and choose our response intentionally. Emotions need to be acknowledged, felt, and given the space to fulfill their purpose, which is to make us *feel*. They are not there to override our rational thought but to provide valuable insight into what's happening within us. Once we've allowed ourselves to experience those feelings, we can then step back and make a conscious decision about how to move forward. This process not only helps us regulate our emotions but also enables us to lead and live with greater intentionality.

For many of us, there are certain people in our lives who seem to have a unique ability to bump up against our wounds. They evoke reactions that feel outsized or disproportionate, throwing us off course and leaving us questioning why we feel so unsettled. More often than not, this is because their words, actions, or presence touch a part of us that feels vulnerable, unhealed, or raw. These moments can feel deeply uncomfortable, but they are also opportunities for growth and self-awareness.

When someone triggers this kind of emotional reaction, it's easy to blame them for how we feel or to let the intensity of the moment dictate our response, but wisdom invites us to approach these situations differently. Instead of reacting impulsively, we can pause and ask ourselves questions like, *why am I feeling this way? What is this person bumping up against in me? How can I respond in a way that aligns with my values and not just my emotions?* This process allows us to reclaim control over our actions, even in situations that feel emotionally charged.

The truth is, emotions are powerful, but they don't have to control us. They are signals, not commands—indicators of what's happening internally, rather than directives for what we should do next. By acknowledging and understanding the emotions that arise when our wounds are touched, we gain the ability to respond thoughtfully rather than react instinctively. This doesn't mean suppressing or ignoring our emotions; it means using them as tools to deepen our understanding of ourselves and to guide us toward wise and intentional choices.

In relationships, particularly with those who provoke strong emotional responses, this approach is transformative. Instead of being derailed by emotional spikes, we can use those moments to learn more about our wounds, our boundaries, and the patterns in our interactions. Over time, this practice helps us build resilience, foster healthier relationships, and navigate life's challenges with greater clarity and grace.

Asking questions can be one of the most powerful tools for building intimacy, not only with others but also with ourselves and our wounds. For me, one of my biggest emotional triggers is encountering someone who acts like a bully. When I see someone doing something I perceive as an "injustice," it immediately bumps up against my wound. I know this because my reaction is visceral. I begin to seethe with anger. My thoughts spiral. My disdain for that person can grow to the point where I can't even look at them without feeling rage. In my younger years, this reaction often led to rude comments or outright verbal confrontations. My default response to my wound being touched was to lash out in defense or retaliation.

But as I've grown, I've begun to approach these moments differently. While the trigger still challenges me deeply, I've learned to pause, take a step back, and process my feelings. I've learned that my initial anger, while real, doesn't have to define my response. Instead of reacting impulsively, I've chosen to lean into empathy and curiosity. Today, when I encounter someone I perceive as a bully, I often ask myself, *What hurt them so badly to make them act this way?*

This shift—from seething to questioning—is a gift of wisdom, and it's transformed how I engage with others. Asking this question doesn't mean I condone bullying or excuse harmful behavior. It means I'm choosing to see the person behind the actions, to recognize that their behavior likely stems from a wound of their own. This simple act of curiosity allows me to move from anger to sadness, from judgment to empathy. It humanizes the person I once wanted to dehumanize, and it opens the door for connection and understanding where there was once only division.

This process of asking questions also fosters intimacy with myself. By questioning my reaction—*Why does this bother me so much? What does this tell me about my own wound?*—I gain deeper insight into my triggers and how they shape my emotions and behavior. Each time I ask these questions, I grow closer to understanding the parts of myself that are still tender and vulnerable. This self-awareness not only helps me navigate my own emotions but also equips me to respond to others with greater grace and wisdom.

When we choose to ask questions instead of reacting, we invite intimacy into our relationships. We show others—and ourselves—that we are willing to go deeper, to seek understanding rather than judgment, and to engage with the complexity of the human experience. This kind of intimacy requires humility and courage, but it's one of the most Christ-like ways we can relate to others. Jesus Himself often asked questions that invited people into deeper self-reflection and connection, showing us that true intimacy begins when we move beyond assumptions and seek the heart of the matter. For me, this shift in perspective is nothing short of a gift from God, and I am profoundly grateful for the wisdom it brings. While I don't always get it right, I know that when I choose to ask questions and respond with empathy, I'm closer to transforming into the person God is calling me to be.

The more you grow intimate with the things that challenge your inner-being, the more you'll be able to handle them with grace, empathy, and curiosity. The wisest people I know don't have uncontrolled emotional reactions; they are measured and cool under pressure. That type of response doesn't happen by accident, and it doesn't happen without work—it happens because of intentional responses woven into the fabric of a person's heart.

The theologian and author John Mark Comer, in his book *Practicing the Way*, suggests that one of the major catalysts for spiritual growth is the practice of solitude. Solitude, as he describes it, is the intentional act of being alone to focus on one's relationship with God. It's not about isolation or withdrawal from the world but about creating a sacred space where you can quiet the noise, reflect, and tune your heart to the voice of the Creator. I deeply resonate with John Mark's perspective, and I'd take it a step further: Solitude isn't just about deepening your relationship with

God—it's also about becoming more aware of what's happening within yourself so that you can be more intentional in how you express who you are externally.

Solitude is where self-awareness and spiritual growth meet. In the quiet moments spent with God, we begin to notice the patterns of our thoughts, the stirrings of our emotions, and the tender places where our wounds still need healing. It's in solitude that we can listen to the Spirit without distraction, gaining clarity about what matters most and how to align our actions with our faith. This internal work equips us to move through the world with purpose and grace, making intentional choices rather than reacting impulsively to the chaos around us.

Daily disciplines like solitude and reading Scripture are the foundation upon which wise people build their lives. These practices ground us, creating a rhythm that prioritizes connection with God and cultivates wisdom. When we anchor ourselves in these disciplines, we gain the perspective that not everything demands our immediate attention or response. Solitude teaches us that we don't have to react to someone else's irrational behavior or be drawn into every conflict. It gives us the space to discern what truly requires our energy and what can be released without comment or action.

In a world that often rewards quick reactions and constant engagement, this kind of restraint is countercultural—but it's also transformative. As the police famously say, *"You have the right to remain silent."* From my perspective, the wisest among us exercise that right diligently. They understand that silence, when rooted in wisdom, is not weakness but strength. It's the strength to choose patience over impulsivity, reflection over retaliation, and peace over unnecessary conflict. Solitude trains us in this discipline, teaching us to trust that God is at work even when we choose not to speak or act.

The practice of solitude isn't just a tool for spiritual growth—it's a way of life that shapes how we show up in the world. It reminds us that everything has its place and time, and not every moment requires our intervention. In solitude, we learn to listen more than we speak, to observe more than we react, and to trust more than we control. This is the wisdom that grows in the quiet, and it's a gift that overflows into every area of life.

Several years ago, the Lord gave me a sentence that has become a guiding principle in my life and leadership—a sentence I often share on my podcast because of its profound impact: **If you aren't dedicated to your disciplines, you'll be destroyed by your distractions.** This simple yet powerful truth has shaped much of my spiritual and emotional walk as a leader. It's a reminder that the foundation of who we are is built on the practices we prioritize daily. Disciplines aren't just routines; they are the habits that mold us into the people we aspire to be, equipping us to navigate the complexities of life with clarity and purpose.

The daily practices we commit to—whether they involve physical health, spiritual growth, or emotional well-being—have a ripple effect on every area of our lives. For instance, if I skip going to the gym or neglect moving my body, I notice a shift in my emotional disposition. I may feel more irritable, less focused, or even disconnected from myself. Similarly, when I fail to spend time in solitude or immerse myself in Scripture, it affects my spiritual and emotional grounding. The absence of these practices leaves me feeling untethered, more vulnerable to distractions, and less capable of handling life's challenges with wisdom.

These disciplines are not just about ticking boxes; they are formative. They create the mental, emotional, and spiritual space we need to become intimate with our wounds and gifts. Without daily disciplines, we can easily go through life reacting rather than reflecting and numbing rather than noticing. As leaders and followers of Christ, this is especially dangerous because it's in these moments of discipline—solitude, Scripture, prayer, exercise, or reflection—that we gain the clarity to recognize what's happening within us. As the saying goes, *you can't see what you don't make time to look at.* If we neglect these practices, our wounds remain in the shadows, influencing our actions in ways we don't even realize.

When we start our day rushed or behind, we are already at a disadvantage. The absence of intentionality in the morning often carries over into the rest of the day, making it harder to respond with wisdom or grace. Distractions creep in, pulling us in a hundred different directions, and before we know it, we're exhausted, frustrated, or overwhelmed. Dedication to discipline protects us from this spiral. It grounds us, giving us the tools to face the day with focus and resilience.

The beauty of discipline is that it creates freedom—not the freedom to do whatever we want but the freedom to become who God is calling us to be. It gives us the strength to see our wounds, the courage to address them, and the wisdom to live in alignment with our values. When we are dedicated to our disciplines, we are actively participating in the work of becoming more Christ-like, equipping ourselves to lead, love, and serve with clarity and purpose.

In the recovery community, there is an old saying: "You'll never make a good decision when you are in a H.A.L.T. scenario." Halt means hungry, angry, lonely, tired. When you are feeling those things, you need to HALT what you are doing and reevaluate the situation. Self-awareness as a leader is knowing the ins and outs of your physical, emotional, and spiritual disposition so that you can lead well. Even the wisest people in the world get tired; they just know that when they are tired, they need to sleep not have serious conversations about decisions that need to be made. Far too often, we put ourselves in a situation where it is even harder to be successful than on a normal day by not acknowledging what we are bringing into the moment.

A practical example of this in my own life is Sunday morning on the Sundays when I teach/preach. When I am giving a message, I am giving an emotional part of myself to the congregation. I'm prepared, I'm present, and I'm doing the best I can. Regardless of how the message goes, I'm still pouring myself out to my community. Where that leads to problems is when someone tries to talk to me in between services. A very kind and loving church member might come up and ask for me to pray for someone or to send them something, and to be honest, there is no chance I'm going to remember that. I promise you I'm going to forget everything you ask me on a Sunday morning when I'm teaching. I used to be embarrassed about this, but when I learned that I can be honest, everything changed. I realized that if I just tell people I won't remember this and to send me a follow up email, two things happened: I received tons of grace, and a lot of those folks never sent emails.

Wisdom is awareness—the kind of deep understanding that comes from taking an honest and intentional look at who you are. This awareness doesn't happen by accident; it requires effort, reflection, and a commitment to self-discovery. Wisdom isn't just about knowledge or intellect; it's about knowing yourself—your strengths, your weaknesses, your wounds, and your gifts—and using that knowledge to navigate life with purpose and integrity. When you cultivate this awareness, you're better equipped to handle challenges, build meaningful relationships, and make decisions that align with your values.

To grow in awareness, you have to take the time to learn who you are. This means exploring what motivates you, what triggers you, and what you care about most deeply. It also means facing the parts of yourself that are uncomfortable or unhealed—the wounds that influence how you think, feel, and act. This kind of self-reflection isn't always easy, but it's essential for growth. It's in knowing yourself that you begin to unlock the wisdom to live authentically and lead effectively.

When in doubt, one of the most transformative things you can do is to be honest—honest about where you are and how you're feeling. Honesty invites connection, both with yourself and others. It breaks down the walls of pretense and perfectionism, creating space for growth and understanding. When you're honest about your struggles, emotions, and doubts, you're able to address them with clarity and intention. It also fosters trust in your relationships, showing others that it's okay to be real, vulnerable, and human.

This combination—awareness, discipline, and honesty—has the power to change everything. It helps you move through life with purpose rather than reaction, and it equips you to face challenges with resilience and grace. Wisdom isn't about having all the answers; it's about being intentional in how you seek them, how you live, and how you lead. When you take the time to cultivate awareness, build disciplines, and embrace honesty, you lay the foundation for a life of deeper meaning, stronger relationships, and lasting impact.

Exercise:

1. Gift Identification Workshop:

- With your team or a group you lead, ask each person to list their strengths and passions.

- Facilitate a discussion about how these strengths contribute to the group's goals and how they align with individual gifts.

2. Mentoring Exercise:

- Identify one person you lead who may need help discovering their gift. Schedule a one-on-one conversation to explore their strengths, wounds, and areas of fulfillment. Walk alongside them in their journey to becoming a more courageous leader.

- Share an example of how your own wound led to you recognizing your gift and how that might inspire them.

3. Gift Integration Plan:

- For a specific project or goal, align team members' roles with their gifts.

- Encourage them to reflect on how their contributions make a difference and how they feel when operating from their gift.

Epilogue

The Art of Conscious Leadership

As you close this book, take a moment to reflect on the beauty and complexity of your journey. Leadership, as we've explored, is not just a practice or a skill; it is an art. It's the art of being fully present, embracing your wounds, and letting God's redemptive power transform them into gifts.

In 2 Corinthians 12:9, Paul reminds us of this truth: *"But he said to me, 'My grace is sufficient for you, for my power is made perfect in weakness.' Therefore I will boast all the more gladly about my weaknesses, so that Christ's power may rest on me."* This is the paradox of leadership—our weaknesses and our wounds are not barriers but bridges to God's grace and strength.

To lead consciously means to approach your emotions, challenges, and relationships with grace and humility. It requires sitting in your feelings, acknowledging their presence, and letting them reveal the deeper truths about who you are. Just as Jesus wept at the tomb of Lazarus (John 11:35), showing the depth of His humanity and love, we too are invited to feel deeply. Emotions are not signs of weakness but invitations to grow closer to God, to others, and to ourselves.

Give yourself grace. Grace to feel. Grace to fail. Grace to try again. Leadership, like art, is not about perfection but authenticity. It's about letting the Holy Spirit guide you through the messiness of life and transform your wounds into a canvas of redemption and beauty.

Leading With Authenticity

Authentic leadership requires vulnerability, and vulnerability can be scary. It asks us to let others see the real us, wounds and all. But it is precisely in this space that true connection and influence are born. When we lead with authenticity, we invite others into a relationship built on trust, empathy, and mutual respect.

Take time to consider the areas of your leadership where you've struggled to be fully transparent. Are there wounds you've hidden, believing they disqualify you? Or moments of failure you've buried, fearing they might undermine your credibility? What if, instead, those very things could be the key to unlocking deeper connections with those you lead?

Remember Moses, who doubted his ability to lead because of his stutter (Exodus 4:10). Yet, God used Moses' perceived weakness to show His strength. He reminded Moses—and us—that leadership is not about perfection but about obedience and faith. What weaknesses in your life might God be inviting you to surrender so He can use them to demonstrate His power?

The Art of Sitting in Your Feelings

One of the hardest things about conscious leadership is learning to sit in your feelings. Our natural instinct is often to push past uncomfortable emotions, to ignore the pain and move forward. But emotions are not obstacles to avoid; they are teachers to learn from.

When we sit in our feelings, we honor the way God created us. We allow ourselves to experience the fullness of our humanity, while also inviting God to meet us in our vulnerability. This is not a passive process. It requires courage to face what we feel and wisdom to discern what those feelings are revealing about our hearts.

Consider Jesus in the Garden of Gethsemane (Matthew 26:36–39). He felt deep anguish and sorrow, yet He didn't run from those emotions. Instead, He brought them to the Father, asking for strength and submitting to His will. What would it look like for you to bring your emotions to God, trusting Him to provide the clarity and courage you need to move forward?

Grace in Leadership

Leadership often feels like a balancing act. We strive to inspire, support, and guide others while managing our own insecurities, emotions, and imperfections. In the midst of this tension, it is easy to become self-critical, measuring ourselves against impossible standards. But grace reminds us that we don't have to have it all figured out.

Grace allows us to embrace the reality that we are works in progress. It frees us from the pressure to perform and instead invites us to lead from a place of authenticity and humility. When we give ourselves grace, we also model it for others, creating a culture where imperfection is not only accepted but celebrated as a catalyst for growth.

Your Wounds Are Not the End of Your Story

As you reflect on your journey, remember that your wounds are not the end of your story. They are a part of your story, yes, but they do not sentence you. Instead, they point to God's redemptive work in your life.

In Romans 8:28, we are reminded that *"...God works for the good of those who love him, who have been called according to his purpose."* Your wounds, no matter how deep, are not wasted. They are tools in the hands of a loving Creator who is shaping you into the leader you were always meant to be.

Think about the lessons your wounds have taught you. How have they shaped your perspective, strengthened your resilience, or deepened your empathy? Reflect on the ways God has used your pain to bring healing and hope to others. Your story is a testament to His grace, and your willingness to embrace it is a gift to the world.

Moving Forward with Courage

Leadership is not a destination; it is a journey. It is a continual process of learning, growing, and becoming. As you move forward, commit to leading with courage—the courage to be vulnerable, to embrace your wounds, and to trust God's redemptive work in your life.

Take practical steps to integrate what you've learned into your daily life. Create rhythms of reflection, seeking regular opportunities to sit with your emotions and explore their deeper truths. Surround yourself with a community of support, people who can speak truth into your life and help you navigate the challenges of leadership. Most importantly, stay rooted in your relationship with God, allowing His grace to guide and sustain you.

The Invitation to Legacy

Finally, consider the legacy you want to leave as a leader. Legacy is not about accomplishments or accolades; it is about impact. It is about the lives you touch, the values you instill, and the hope you inspire. By leading consciously and authentically, you have the opportunity to create a ripple effect of grace, love, and transformation that extends far beyond yourself.

What kind of leader do you want to be remembered as? What values do you want to pass on to the next generation? Reflect on these questions, and let them shape your approach to leadership moving forward.

Be courageous. His grace is sufficient. Your gift awaits.

SCAN HERE to learn more about
Invite Ministries—created to invite people to a deeper
faith and living relationship with Jesus Christ